TWO ONE ACT PLAYS BY GABRIEL MARCEL

Dot the I and The Double Expertise

Translated by

Katharine Rose Hanley

Introduction by

Jean-Marie and Anne Marcel

To Bob,
with fond remembrance
and admiring regard.
Katharine Rose Hanley

UNIVERSITY PRESS OF AMERICA

LANHAM • NEW YORK • LONDON

University Press of America,® Inc.

4720 Boston Way
Lanham, MD 20706

3 Henrietta Street
London WC2E 8LU England

Printed in the United States of America

Library of Congress Cataloging in Publication Data

Marcel, Gabriel, 1889-1973.
Two one act plays.

Translation of: Les points sur les i, and of: La double expertise.
Bibliography: p.
Contents: Dot the I—The double expertise.
1. Marcel, Gabriel, 1889-1973—Translations, English.
I. Marcel, Gabriel, 1889-1973. Double expertise.
English. 1985 II. Title.
PQ2645.A755A24 1985 842'.912 85-22571
ISBN 0-8191-5076-2 (alk paper)
ISBN 0-8191-5077-0 (pbk. : alk. paper)

ACKNOWLEDGEMENTS

I wish to thank Monsieur and Madame Jean-Marie and Anne Marcel for their generous friendship, significant help, and constant encouragement from the beginnings of this project through to its completion.

I also wish to acknowledge Editions Albin Michel´s kind permission to publish these English versions of Dot the I and The Double Expertise for which they hold copyrights to the original French texts Les points sur les I and La Double Expertise that were published along with Colombyre ou le brasier de la paix and Le Divertissement posthume in Théâtre comique, Paris, Editions Albin Michel, 1947.

To the officers, members, and friends of the International Association Présence de Gabriel Marcel and the Gabriel Marcel Institute for Existential Drama of Le Moyne College I wish to express sincere gratitude for their enthusiastic support of this project.

TABLE OF CONTENTS

INTRODUCTION

"Probably it is quite natural," wrote Gabriel Marcel in 1964, "that having reached the age that I have today, I feel the need to ask myself about my work, especially in the respect that it is both complex and even apparently incongruous.

"In my philosophic writings I said what I wanted to say. In principle, philosophic thought is transparent to itself. For poetry, and especially for dramatic poetry, the situation is quite different. In this latter case the words ´wanted to say´ no longer have the precise meaning they have for the philosopher. I would not even hesitate to say that a certain nonintentionality is distinctive of any dramatic creation worthy of the name.

"One characteristic of my dramatic work that I feel I should stress is its original quality. I can say that I yielded to a sort of urge that I had felt since childhood. In contrast to this, at least in my case, philosophic work was secondary, which doesn´t mean that my earliest efforts at playwriting didn´t show a certain childishness that still astounds me today.

"The creative urge expressed itself, I would say, in giving rise to imagined characters. It was a question of a need not to talk about people but rather to let them speak for themselves, and to show how they reacted to each other.

"I believe I can recognize today that at the origin of my passion for theater there was also a need to escape, a need to get away from the solitude of being an only child, one whose life was too scrutinized, living among adults who were too preoccupied with my physical and moral development and who let nothing of what I could do or feel go unnoticed.

"I am thus led to think that from very early on, and without really being conscious of it, I sought by way of reaction to hide myself in characters very different from me.

"What is clear, in any event, is that this passion for dialogue signaled well in advance the concern for the ´thou´ or the philosophy of intersubjectivity that I was to articulate many years later.

"In my plays, an important element is the development of a sort of ´constructive modulation, one that introduces or is oriented toward a reconciling harmony. But how can a playwright abstract from everything in this life as it is given to us, that presents itself as discord and cacophony? Without a doubt, my comic theater corresponds to a deeply felt need to let these discordant voices be heard. . . ."

These lines, part of an allocution preceding the performance of a play by Gabriel Marcel at Saarebruck in Germany, show the importance the dramatic works and in particular the comedies held for their author, an importance equal to that of his philosophic writings, which are another mode of expression drawn from a unique source.

Theater was an important part of Gabriel Marcel´s life. He loved theater passionately. Right up to the very last years of his life he went to see two or three plays each week. For many years he was a drama critic whose reviews had authority and influence; his weekly reviews were anxiously awaited by directors, actors and actresses, and authors alike.

When a play he had authored had been selected and was being staged in a theater, he lived feverishly. There were first the auditions and the casting, then the rehearsals, actors or actresses who didn´t know their lines, a director who was too harsh or not firm enough, and then all those discoveries one makes about one´s own work: its high points that are striking, those moments where interest lags--and to whose account must these be laid, an actor or actress, the director, or oneself, the author? Then there is the rhythm that establishes itself and the pace that quickens as rehearsals progress, actors and actresses get more into roles and perform better and better, for actors and actresses always improve, never the reverse.

And then it´s the final rehearsal, the semipublic "dress rehearsal"; finally the "preview" for the critics, a terrible ordeal (will they like it?), and then at last "opening night" for all Paris, one´s friends, the general public whose reviews can be as pitiless as those of the professional critics. But what unsurpassable joy if one feels that he is understood, if one sees that others are moved by characters in whom one has put a bit of oneself, if one has succeeded in communicating something vital and important.

Just a week or so before the opening of one of his plays, Le Chemin de Crête (Ariadne in the English version), Gabriel Marcel was a victim of a serious automobile accident that left him with a fractured hip. He insisted he be brought to the theater on a stretcher. . . .

Gabriel Marcel was perhaps more attached to his theater even than to his philosophy. Whenever one of his plays was being staged in Germany, Belgium, England, or elsewhere, he was anxious to be there personally to attend the performance and to congratulate the actors and actresses. No longer was he the pitiless critic; he would be completely caught up in enthusiasm. How happy he would be today to see the English versions so well translated by Ms. Katharine Rose Hanley; without any hesitation he would board an airplane and fly to a performance, delighted to see characters whom he´d carried in his head become enfleshed in the bodies, voices, and language of very lively young Americans.

Yes, doubtless that would have been a joy for him, as it is also for us his children, and we are very happy to congratulate Ms. Hanley for her excellent work and for the friendship and the fidelity it demonstrates.

Ten years ago, the friends of Gabriel Marcel formed an International Association,[1] and this tenth anniversary will be marked by the publication of several important works in Paris, the letters of Gabriel Marcel and Gaston Fessard will appear, edited with an introduction by Henri Cardinal de Lubac, and Gabriel Marcel´s correspondence with the Swiss philosopher Max Picard will also be published; in Canada, a critical study of Gabriel Marcel´s philosophic vocabulary by Simone Plourde will appear. But we are especially happy to think that in the United States of America Gabriel Marcel´s work is becoming more widely known in its theatrical dimension, to wit, his comic theater. That there are still in our times people throughout the world who know how to enjoy a good hearty laugh is indeed a hopeful sign.

Jean-Marie and Anne Marcel

[1] 85 boulevard de Port-Royal, 75013 Paris, France

Translator's Preface

As it was a great joy to see Dot the I and The Double Expertise performed on stage in 1977 and 1978, so it is an equally great joy now to see these two plays published in English versions, so that others can read them and eventually experience them as staged dramas.

Until recently, Gabriel Marcel's theater was scarcely known to an English-speaking audience, since only a few plays have been translated from the original French. In the William James Lectures that Marcel delivered at Harvard University in 1961, he expressed the hope that an English-speaking audience would soon have the opportunity of becoming familiar with his theater.[1]

Two One Act Plays: Dot the I and The Double Expertise brings to a total of nine the number of Gabriel Marcel's thirty plays available in English versions. The British Broadcasting Company commissioned translations that were published in Three Plays by Gabriel Marcel: Ariadne, A Man of God and The Votive Candle or The Funeral Pyre. Joseph Cunneen, with Elizabeth Stambler, translated The Lantern, a one act play that was commissioned for La Comédie Française and published it in Cross Currents magazine. The Unfathomable, the first act of an unfinished play, was published in Presence and Immortality. The Broken World and The Rebellious Heart appeared in The Existential Drama of Gabriel Marcel, edited by Francis J. Lescoe in 1974.[2]

The two plays selected for this volume, Dot the I and The Double Expertise, not only increase the number of Marcel's plays that are now available to an English-speaking audience; they also enable an English-speaking public to taste Marcel's comic theater and thus have a more balanced perception of his theatrical production that includes both comic and tragic plays. These two one act plays are representative of the style of Marcel's theater. Dot the I reveals the poignancy of his dramatic art, and The Double Expertise shows the full gamut of his gift as a comic writer.

Dot the I presents three liberal-minded adults who are attempting to live a three-way marriage. This household includes Anatole Girondin, a playwright who hopes his creative genius will soon be acknowledged; Irma, who is a live-in mistress and muse for Anatole's inspiration; and Anatole's wife Felicia, who keeps house for them all. Also with them is Aimee, Irma's daughter who came to join her mother in Paris when Aimee's father no longer had room for her with him in the South of France.

The play lets the audience experience the struggles these three adults endure as they strive to succeed with their "noble experiment" that far surpassess the narrow-minded limits of what society's conformists could imagine.

The unfolding of the play's action reveals mounting tension. The strain on relationships reaches a breaking point when the wife, ironically named Felicia, learns that Irma and Anatole, passing themselves off as Mr. and Mrs. Girondin, are going for a weekend in the country, at the home of a socially prominent couple who could be influential in arranging to have Robespierre, Anatole's latest play, produced at the National Theater. Furious at this development, Felicia protests, but in vain. Then, beside herself in desperation, she sends Aimee to run after Irma and company to their car to tell her mother that Felicia says she is going to give her a full and complete explanation of the whole situation. "Tell your mother," Felicia says, "that I am going to dot the i's."[3]

When the child returns to the apartment, the living room has been darkened, the drapes are drawn, and only one electric lamp is lit. It appears that all is set for Aimee to hear the harsh facts of life and to learn the cruel truth that she is unloved and unwanted, and certainly she cannot count on staying there much longer.

As the conversation between Felicia and Aimee progresses, it takes some surprising turns, as does the direction in which the action of the play develops. Dot the I has an ending that is dramatically powerful and quite unexpected.

Without giving away the surprise ending or revealing too much of the story line of Dot the I, a few more remarks can be made about some characteristics of Gabriel Marcel's theater.

In The Theater Hour, a book of drama criticism, Marcel observed that a play's last act is what gives the play its unity and its enduring quality. He notes further that the last act, particularly the last scene, is also important for the questions it raises.[4]

Dot the I raises questions that tend to remain with the audience after the play's end. These questions refer to the play's characters but engage the lives of the spectators as well. One question that arises is, "What does it mean to dot the i's?"[5] The play also leaves spectators wondering whether anyone can dot the i's or cross the t's about the meaning of interpersonal relations. One wonders whether one can give that kind of clear-cut, matter of fact, almost definitive explanation to an interaction of freedoms or to the sense of people's lives. After the audience has heard the varying interpretations of the situation at the Girondin household, one wonders whether anyone sees the situation in the light of truth. As the play ends, one even wonders what it might be like to see and understand things in the light of truth. One wonders how someone could come to a perspective of understanding where lucidity and compassion merge and where freedom is enhanced.

Marcel´s plays most often have surprise endings. Rather than a denouement that settles problems and puts everyone neatly in their proper places, Marcel plays often end on a note of dissonance that invites further reflection. The end of the play has a puzzling or haunting effect. It raises questions that require or invite the spectator to reconstruct the play in reverse, rethinking it in the light of these questions and even sometimes researching these same issues as they occur in one´s own life.

Marcel´s plays examine questions, very concretely investigating how they affect the lives of individuals in situations that can be familiar to us all. Yet his theater seems not only to portray the concrete events and circumstances, but also seems to convey what the individual characters are living "within." Thus Marcel´s dramas present lifelike characters, who not only share with audiences what they are living--as they come to consciousness of the tragic dimension in their life situations--but characters who also reveal something of who they are and what they live by. This certainly occurs, quite clearly and powerfully, in the case of Dot the I.

On the one hand, Dot the I, while it does include comic aspects and moments of definite humor and wit, is definitely characterized by an atmosphere that carries a certain sadness and an ending that has serious depth. On the other hand, The Double Expertise is a much more light-hearted comedy. The Double Expertise is a satirical farce that presents the humorous developments and surprises that occur as family and friends, with all their flaws and foibles, get involved in a ridiculously funny match-making scene.

The Double Expertise takes place in an elegant bachelor´s apartment in Paris in the mid-1930s. This is the home of Gilbert Marquiset, who is contemplating marriage for a third time. Since he is not overconfident about his judgment in such matters, he invites his first wife, Georgette, to come and help him evaluate the prospective bride-to-be. Georgette arrives accompanied by her second husband, Stani Zurcher. She wants him there because now he and she think alike and try to decide everything together. As these three are comparing successive domestic economies and trying to estimate the qualities of this third prospect, an unexpected interruption occurs. Kate Leliegois, Gil´s second estranged wife, arrives. She comes to claim something as collateral for Gil´s alimony payments which are long overdue. When she learns the purpose of the others´ gathering, she claims the right to stay and vote as part of the jury. Just then, Hedwig Fruhling, a Swiss Miss, arrives, accompanied by her uncle, an appraiser with a double expertise. There follows a comedy of errors as concealed identities are revealed and embarrassingly overlapping relationships are unveiled.

Gil introduces Georgette and Stani Zurcher (his former first wife and her second husband) as "cousins." He presents Kate (his estranged second wife) as "a distant relative." In astonishment Stani exclaims, "Father," when he sees Mr. Ed Zurcher enter with Ms. Hedwig Fruhling. Later it becomes clear that Stani and his father became estranged over the settlement of Stani´s mother´s inheritance. As both parties, Gilbert and Hedwig, attempt to evaluate the proposed merger, one by a jury´s vote, the other by an expert´s appraisal, their schemes and identities are unmasked and their purposes flounder. Even Hedwig´s scene of conducting a group recollection to bring about a consensus fails ludicrously.

The play´s denouement is a tragic/comic fiasco. One after another the jury, (Georgette and Stani), the claimant (Kate with her security, a Dufy painting, in hand), and the appraiser (disenchanted with everything he´s seen) all leave. An ambitious plan for union ends in the helter-skelter disarray of retreat. But just as it appears that the ridiculous plan has failed totally, there is a surprise development and a reversal of direction. The play ends on an ironic note of question.

At the play´s end it is not clear whether or not Gil and Hedwig will marry. That issue is still an open question, as are the issues of whether there are reliable grounds for matrimony and whether there exist essential criteria that would enable family and friends--perhaps even the couple themselves--to evaluate whether this proposed match is likely to become a good and lasting marriage. These issues come to light through the concrete action of the play. <u>The Double Expertise</u>´s surprise ending and the attitude of questioning it awakens incite the audience to search for light on these questions both by researching the play--reconstructing it in their minds in the light of the questions that linger hauntingly after the play´s end--and by questioning these issues in relationship to one´s own experience, thoughts, and feelings.

<u>The Double Expertise</u> is a cleverly amusing comedy, an effective satirical farce. Yet as the play ends on an ironic note of dissonance, it has a haunting effect. Just as in the case of <u>Dot the I,</u> the ending of <u>The Double Expertise</u> raises questions and invites reflection on how those questions refer to

the characters of the play and how they refer to the lives of members of the audience.

Marcel noted that his comedies reflect the "yes, but. . ." character of his thought. Marcel had a very balanced life view. He was keenly aware of the presence of both the tragic and the comic in the human condition, and well aware also of the ambiguity in any human personality. His comic theater portrays our hopes and our fears, our nobility and our foolishness, in satirical or burlesque fashion. His comic art has a certain magic that lets audiences perceive two sides of the same coin, both the comic and tragic aspects of a situation. By portraying the comic aspects, Marcel seems also to highlight the serious dimension of the issues at stake.

The ironic and perplexing endings of Marcel's plays, especially his comedies, reflect his refusal to accept pat answers to the challenging issues of life. Life's mysteries, he found, were best clarified when individuals reflected upon their own life experiences, and freely responded to the infinite richness and light available there.[6]

The two one act plays by Gabriel Marcel, Dot the I and The Double Expertise, present the dramatic situations that develop as people's lives are affected by certain crucial events. These dramas heighten consciousness of the issues involved. They bring to light certain questions and perspectives of insight, and they invite further reflective clarification and consideration of paths opened up for freedom to explore.

It often happened that, ten or fifteen years after writing a play, Marcel would reflect philosophically upon its questions and explicitly clarify their significance through reasoned analysis. Some of the perspectives brought to light in Dot the I were treated thematically about ten years later in an essay, "Testimony and Existentialism," in The Philosophy of Existentialism. Similarly, some of the questions raised by The Double Expertise were investigated philosophically in Creative Fidelity, written a good ten years after the plays that inspired some of its perspectives of inquiry.[7]

Marcel was in the unique and somewhat paradoxical situation of having two full-fledged and autonomous vocations. He pursued each according to its own appropriate method and purpose. Yet, given the integrity of the man, and the highly personal character of his work, there is a complementarity between his theater and philosophy.

It is important to understand this complementarity correctly. The plays were created first, as concrete imaginings of the dramatic possibilities developing from seeing particular individuals in a given situation of conflict or challenge. The philosophic writings followed, often much later, as rigorous, critically reasoned reflections on some of the questions or issues that dramatic situations first brought to light.

Marcel's plays were not written to illustrate philosophic ideas, even less to argue or proselytize them. The plays portray the influence of significant events in people's lives, and also show their growing awareness of the tragic dimension in their lives.

Gabriel Marcel (1889-1973) was an exceptionally gifted person. He was a playwright and a philosopher, and he worked regularly for over forty years as a drama critic. He also improvised musical compositions for piano, usually to bring some of his favorite poems to full expression in song. Marcel received many national and international honors and awards, among others a Grand Prize of Literature conferred by the French Academy and the Frankfurt Peace Prize for one who has promoted human dignity and kinship beyond national frontiers.

For Gabriel Marcel, theater and philosophy were two autonomous and full-fledged vocations. He wrote more than thirty plays. One of these is in the permanent repertory of the Comédie Française, and most of the others were produced in major theaters in France and other countries as well. Marcel wrote philosophical conferences, journals, and essays. He has seventeen major books of philosophy, published in French and translated into many other languages. He published three full-length books of drama criticism as well as countless articles, reviews, lectures, and prefaces.[8]

For Marcel, theater and philosophy were distinct and autonomous vocations. He communicated creatively in each, responding to a definite calling and respecting the canons of each discipline. Because of the integrity and unity that characterized his life, and because of the highly personal quality of his thought--both his theater and his philosophy evolved as reflections exploring aspects of questions that arose in his own life--there developed a real complementarity between his works of theater and his essays in philosophy.

Marcel was anxious that his theater be accepted in its own right and that it be evaluated on the basis of its own intrinsic strengths and weaknesses. He was fearful lest people not give a fair hearing to his theater but rather dismiss it as a mere hobby or avocation of a philosopher. He took pains to clarify that his was not a thesis theater, where ideas are argued or illustrated. On the contrary, in his case theater precedes philosophy and the tone is one of exploration, not demonstration.

Marcel´s plays were a first moment of reflective inquiry bringing to the light of the stage his investigation of dramatic situations in people´s lives. Philosophy was always a subsequent moment and level of reflection, one that explored in terms of rational discourse some of the questions and perspectives of inquiry that the action of the dramas had already highlighted. For Marcel, theater and philosophy were complementary modes of inquiry. A careful study of the dates of composition of his various works bears out the fact that theater was the first form of inquiry and philosophy was always a subsequent investigation.

Theater also plays a concretizing role in relationship to Marcel´s philosophy. Marcel felt that issues affecting human lives should be considered in the same manner in which they occur, namely as concrete events affecting the conscious experience of individuals´ lives. Issues affecting the meaning and value of human lives, he felt, should not be argued or debated merely in a theoretical abstract fashion nor with an impersonal, rationalistic approach. Such issues, he thought, should be subject to lucid, critically reasoned analysis and interpretation, but they should be reflectively clarified in relation to the real context in which they occur, namely the life experience of people who are affected by them. Theater shows the way life´s challenges, conflicts, and questions touch people´s lives concretely. Dramas portray how people´s lives are affected incarnately, that is bodily, spiritually, affectively, and consciously by life´s crucial events. Since the theater shows people´s responses to the impact of significant events that affect their lives, it can be a highly valuable if not indispensable way of access to Marcel´s philosophic reflection.

Once the prospective and concretizing roles of theater in relationship to philosophy are accurately understood, the complementarity between Gabriel Marcel´s theater and philosophy can readily be appreciated. Marcel observed that for him theater and philosophy were like two faces of the same mountain climbed, or two slopes of the same height scaled. Theater and philosophy can also be viewed as the landscape and countryside on either side of the one road traveled.

Marcel observed that the importance different individuals will attach to his theater or to his philosophy will probably depend to a significant extent upon each individual´s preference. Yet Marcel pointed out that he himself, especially toward the end of his life, felt closest to his theater. There he always found fresh, lively inspiration, and theater is where he best recognized himself for the spirit of compassion and real fraternity that resonates and says "you are understood."

I consider it a privilege to have worked on the translations and stage productions of these two one act plays by Gabriel Marcel, Dot the I and The Double Expertise. The translations of both these plays were done in the process of stage productions, with the idea that this context would help to keep the language lively and stageworthy. I hope the exigencies of very live actors and audiences have helped to keep the language colloquial, both natural and faithful to the original.

It is a heartening joy to realize that this publication of Two One Act Plays by Gabriel Marcel will introduce an English-speaking audience to a significant part of his theater, for such an encounter can be for many the beginning of a rich and fruitful association.

Katharine Rose Hanley

Footnotes to Translator's Preface

1. Gabriel Marcel, The Existential Background of Human Dignity, The William James Lectures delivered at Harvard University, 1961-62, Cambridge, Mass., Harvard University Press, 1963, 178 p.

2. The Lantern appeared in Cross Currents, Vol. VIII, No. 2, Spring 1958, pp. 129-43; Three Plays by Gabriel Marcel: A Man of God, Ariadne, and The Votive Candle (originally entitled The Funeral Pyre), New York, Hill and Wang, 1965; The Existential Drama of Gabriel Marcel, ed. Francis J. Lescoe, McAuley Institute, St. Joseph College, West Hartford, Connecticut, 1974. The Unfathomable, first act of an unfinished play was published in Presence and Immortality, Pittsburgh, Pa., Duquesne University Press, 1967, pp. 245-84.

3. Dot the I, Lanham, Maryland, University Press of America, 1985, p. 16.

4. L'Heure théâtrale. De Giraudoux à Jean-Paul Sartre, Paris, Plon, 1959, p. xi; Le Secret est dans les îles, Paris, Plon, 1967, p. 20; Preface to Percées vers un ailleurs, Paris, Fayard, 1973, p. 1.; "De la recherche philosophique" in Entretiens autour de Gabriel Marcel, Neuchatel, à la Baconnière, 1976, p. 9.; "Drama of the Soul in Exile" in Three Plays by Gabriel Marcel, New York, Hill and Wang, 1965, p. 30.

5. Dot the I, p. 19.

6. "My Dramatic Works as viewed by the Philosopher," in Searchings, New York, Newman Press, 1967, p. 115.

7. "Testimony and Existentialism," pp. 91-103 in The Philosophy of Existentialism, Secaucus, New Jersey, The Citadel Press, 1956. Creative Fidelity, pp. 38-57, 147-83, New York, Farrar, Straus and Co., 1964.

8. Lists of Gabriel Marcel's major works appear in an appendix as does a brief biblio-biography, pp. 41-58.

   Persons seeking commentary on Gabriel Marcel's theater may read with interest: "The Drama of the Soul in Exile," a preface, pp. 13-34 in Three Plays by Gabriel Marcel, New York, Hill and Wang, 1965; "Introduction" pp. 9-18 in The Existential Drama of Gabriel Marcel, McAuley Institute, St. Joseph College, W. Hartford, Connecticut, 1974; "My Dramatic Works as viewed by the Philosopher," pp. 93-118 in

Searchings , New York, Newman Press, 1967; *The Existential Background of Human Dignity* , Cambridge, Mass., Harvard University Press, 1963; "An Autobiographical Essay," pp. 1-68 in *The Philosophy of Gabriel Marcel* , (Library of Living Philosophers Vol. XVII), ed. P. A. Schilpp and L. E. Hahn, LaSalle, Illinois, Open Court, 1984. Others´ commentaries on Marcel´s theater can be found in Kenneth T. Gallagher´s *The Philosophy of Gabriel Marcel* , New York, Fordham University Press, 1962, 1975, Ch. VII. "The Drama of Communion," pp. 96-115; in Vincent P. Miceli´s *Ascent to Being, Gabriel Marcel´s Philosophy of Communion* , New York, Desclée, 1965, Ch. VII. "Transcendence through Tragedy," pp. 141-93; and in K. R. Hanley´s *Dramatic Approaches to Creative Fidelity,* Lanham, Maryland, University Press of America, forthcoming. Biographical and bibliographical data may also be found in Seymour Cain´s fine little book, *Gabriel Marcel* , Southbend, Indiana, Regnery/Gateway, 1979.

DOT THE I

A One Act Play

by

Gabriel Marcel

Translated by Katharine Rose Hanley

CAST OF CHARACTERS

(in order of appearance)

IRMA

AIMEE

FELICIA GIRONDIN

ANATOLE GIRONDIN

BLANCHE FOUCARD

LUCIEN FOUCARD

DOT THE I
A One Act Play by Gabriel Marcel

The action takes place at the Girondins´ home. A dining room in a small apartment near the center of Paris.

(Felicia finishes clearing the table; she is wearing a housedress and has a handkerchief tied around her head. Irma is stretched out on a couch. Anatole is smoking his pipe. Aimee sits on a chair staring straight ahead.)

IRMA. -- (In a languishing voice) Aimee, will you close that window, please? My neuralgia is beginning to bother me again.

(Aimee closes the window.)

IRMA. -- (Sniffling.) It´s horrible how that odor lasts. Well, it´s just too bad. Please open the window again for a few minutes. That odor is unbearable.

FELICIA. -- What are you talking about?

IRMA. -- Felicia, it´s the third time this week that you´ve served us cauliflower. Yet you know it doesn´t agree with me. One might think you did it intentionally.

FELICIA. -- A well-cooked cauliflower never hurt anyone. It´s all in your imagination.

IRMA.-- Pass me my pills, Aimee.

FELICIA. -- If you are sick, all you have to do is say so. I´ll make you some broth.

IRMA. -- I have a very delicate stomach, Felicia. Not everyone has your good health. But I must keep in good shape.

FELICIA. -- And I´d like to know who in this house ever cared about my health.

ANATOLE. -- Fortunately you never gave us cause to.

FELICIA. -- When my pains come. . .

IRMA.-- I envy you your rheumatism, Felicia. That´s a healthy person´s illness.

FELICIA. -- (Furiously) Too bad we can´t trade.

IRMA. -- You don´t seem to notice odors. I´ve observed that often enough. As for me, some smells are offensive. (To Aimee) Aimee dear, you had better close the window after all. Decidedly it is good not to be too sensitive, one is less vulnerable.

FELICIA. -- Excuse me. Sensitive and obsessive are two different things.

ANATOLE. -- (At the window) There is a storm brewing. I wonder if I will be able to work this afternoon.

IRMA. -- But first, Anatole, remember. . .

ANATOLE. -- Ah! That´s right.

FELICIA. -- What?

IRMA. -- (After having exchanged signals with Anatole) Nothing.

(A pause.)

ANATOLE. -- That´s it. I´ll do as Shakespeare did.

IRMA. -- How´s that?

ANATOLE. -- When my characters reach a certain degree of exaltation, a certain lyric quality, they´ll speak in verse.

IRMA. -- Magnificent!

ANATOLE. -- In that as in other things, the trend must be reversed.

FELICIA. -- For my part, I don´t think it´s a good idea.

ANATOLE. -- I beg of you, Felicia, take that handkerchief off. It´s two o´clock in the afternoon.

FELICIA. -- And after that? I plan to clean my room thoroughly . . . No, I tell you it is not a good idea. A play must be either in poetry or in prose. Otherwise one becomes confused. It´s disturbing. Moreover, I don´t know: in theater, rhymes are out of date.

IRMA. -- (With disdain) Cyrano , you find that outdated.

FELICIA. -- Rostand, that´s a classic.

IRMA. -- Anatole will be a classic.

FELICIA. -- But first of all, Cyrano is entirely in verse, is it not?

ANATOLE. -- Of course, my dear; but one must return to the one true master, Shakespeare.

FELICIA. -- When we went to see Hamlet , somewhere on the outskirts of Paris, I was bored to tears. It´s not worth a yawn.

IRMA. -- Boredom is not a judgment.

FELICIA. -- One does not go to the theater to be bored. Oh, and besides, I say what I think. (Looking at Aimee) There´s a child that would do well to get some fresh air. The way she´s been living since she got here, it´s no surprise she has no appetite. As for me, at my house I want people to eat, do you understand? Your daughter has a papier-mâché complexion.

IRMA. -- I was just like her at that age too, Felicia.

FELICIA. -- I don´t know anything about that. I would see that she gets a bottle of cod liver oil.

IRMA. -- No, I beg of you; just the thought of it makes me sick.

FELICIA. -- It´s not you who is going to drink it.

AIMEE. -- Dear cousin, if you don´t mind, I shall go stretch out on my bed for a while.

FELICIA. -- Do as you wish, my child; but that´s not a good habit.

(Aimee leaves)

FELICIA. -- She persists in calling me "cousin."

IRMA. -- Well, what do you want her to call you, "Felicia"?

FELICIA. -- That´s true! But I´d like to know where she gets off thinking I´m her cousin.

IRMA. -- You can be sure she´s never wondered about that. She´s not a complicated person. (Mockery from Felicia) Now, if you would like to please me, Anatole. . .

FELICIA. -- (In a bitter voice) What?

IRMA. -- You will go get a haircut. And then, your beard, you know I don´t like it anymore. And I don´t like your felt hat either.

FELICIA. -- His hat is perfect, everyone comments on it. It makes him look different from everyone else in the crowd.

IRMA. -- It´s too flashy.

FELICIA. -- A writer shouldn´t look like a bank teller. As for his hair, you´re out of your mind, quite simply. Oh, he could go for a trim. That I can see. But he will keep the beard. I don´t want Toly looking like an American.

IRMA. -- It´s he who should decide.

FELICIA. -- Not at all. First of all, he has no judgment in such matters. When his By the Way was performed four years ago the reviewer from the Figaro mentioned his lion-like air.

IRMA. -- Well now, that is grotesque!

FELICIA. -- I don´t agree.

ANATOLE. -- It remains to be seen.

FELICIA. -- But I have always known Toly with a beard.

IRMA. -- Me too.

FELICIA. -- (With a devastated air) Obviously. It goes without saying.

IRMA. -- But he would be so much better without all that hair.

FELICIA. -- Please, don´t be so gross.

IRMA. -- If he had a hairless face, he would look like a Roman general.

FELICIA. -- I don´t want him to look like a general. . . What´s more, if you think that I´m fooled by you, you are quite wrong. No one will change my Toly.

IRMA. -- You realize, when his Robespierre is performed at the National Theater, you won´t call him "Toly" anymore.

FELICIA. -- I shall call my husband what I will; that is nobody else´s business. Familiarly. . .

IRMA. -- I know you, you just can´t control what you say even in front of strangers. The echo of a rumor is enough to ruin a career. But it´s all the same to you if he becomes the laughing stock of Paris.

FELICIA. -- Now that´s enough.

ANATOLE. -- (Whispering to Irma) Be careful.

FELICIA. -- Another aside. (To Irma) By the way, it´s the second time you have had the audacity to open my mail. (She waves an announcement of death.) The announcement was addressed to Mr. and Mrs. Girondin.

IRMA. -- A printed notice.

FELICIA. -- An announcement of the death of an old friend of the family, my family.

IRMA. -- I wouldn´t have presumed to open a sealed letter.

FELICIA. -- Oh. That would be too much. But this is already too much, much too much. You mustn´t push me too far.

(Anatole and Irma exchange frightened looks)

IRMA. -- (In an uneasy voice) I´ll go get dressed.

(She leaves)

ANATOLE. -- (After having cleared his throat) My dear, I must say that there is something in your attitude that I don´t quite understand--and that doesn´t seem to fit with your admirable generosity.

FELICIA. -- Enough of that generosity bit.

ANATOLE. -- When two years ago, in a situation whose circumstances you certainly have not forgotten. . .

FELICIA. -- Anatole, don´t talk so pompously.

ANATOLE. -- (Annoyed) My dear Felicia, I am not yet, as are some of my contemporaries, to the point of speaking only in interjections.

FELICIA. -- So?

ANATOLE. -- When we agreed with Irma to a style of living that would show, if I may say so, that all three of us are free spirits. . .yes, even in the face of certain middle-class prejudices, we committed ourselves _ipso facto_ . . .

FELICIA. -- Oh, no Latin phrases, if you please.

ANATOLE. -- To preserve in our daily relations, how shall I say, a certain sophistication, without which we would grind the gears horribly?

FELICIA. -- It´s I who grind?

ANATOLE. -- I was speaking of gears.

FELICIA. -- I don´t understand. (Anatole heaves a heavy sigh) Oh! Literature.

ANATOLE. -- It´s not a question of literature, my dear Felicia, but of daily living. Now especially since that young girl is living with us. . .

FELICIA. -- Ah! Now you´re getting to it. How long is she staying here?

ANATOLE. -- Irma must be given the leisure to decide. . .

FELICIA. -- I won´t allow her to become a permanent fixture. One week. Two weeks at most.

ANATOLE. -- Her mother has hopes of finding her a place "au pair," so she can live and work with a family.

FELICIA. -- Indeed. That child doesn´t know how to lift a finger to do any work. She can barely sputter a few words in

English. At her age, I was much sharper. All she´s good for is catching contagious diseases. She´s not pretty, which is not bad. Sometimes it´s even a good thing. But her manner I find a bit underhanded. She´s never direct or outspoken. Besides, suppose she does find a place. Who´ll provide her spending money? Her father won´t give her a cent, he´s already written that.

ANATOLE. -- No, there´s nothing to be expected from that source, not without a lawsuit.

FELICIA. -- A lawsuit. Irma will pay the cost of that? Hey! No, I may be generous but not to that point.

ANATOLE. -- Nevertheless, one can´t just let her starve.

FELICIA. -- Is that my style? Am I one to just let people starve to death?

ANATOLE. -- You are an excellent creature, Felicia. You have already proven that.

FELICIA. -- You don´t have to butter me up. I have my faults; I´m well aware of them. But I have some depth. I´m not bragging. I say it because it is the truth. But as for Irma--

ANATOLE. -- We are not talking about Irma at the moment.

(Felicia moves)

ANATOLE. -- Besides, you complement one another perfectly. A bit like Martha and Mary.

FELICIA. -- (Bitterly) Mary, you sleep there.

ANATOLE. -- Felicia!

FELICIA. -- No. I´ve had enough. You seem to forget that I agreed to a temporary experiment that I can terminate at any time.

ANATOLE. -- Remember. . .

FELICIA. -- Anytime. From one day to the next. And as Irma has no funds. . . or at least she claims that.

ANATOLE. -- I don´t see at all what you´re trying to get to.

FELICIA. -- Me, it´s always been my style to dot the i´s.

ANATOLE. -- The state of material dependence to which Irma has been reduced, precisely obliges us. . .

FELICIA. -- Obliges us? You have no part in it.

ANATOLE. -- Very well then, creates for you the obligation to be even more generous.

FELICIA. -- I warn you that doesn´t work with me. And besides that, why doesn´t she find a job?

ANATOLE. -- What kind of job, Felicia? Irma is an exceptionally gifted woman, marvelously artistic. . .

FELICIA. -- Enough.

ANATOLE. -- But her role in life is first of all to accept the tribute that her beauty earns for her.

FELICIA. -- Hmmph!

ANATOLE. -- And her duty is to furnish the artist, the poet, with the favor of her encouragement.

FELICIA. -- While the others slave from morning until night. Well, thank you no.

ANATOLE. -- Life isn´t just, Felicia, you have to admit that. Life is even cruel. But the wise love that cruelty. Nietzsche, about whom I have reservations in many other respects. . .

FELICIA. -- Let her be a cleaning lady then. I´ll make it my business to find work for her.

ANATOLE. -- You are out of your mind, Felicia. . .I´m far from ignoring, you can be sure, the sacrifices demanded of you by this rather strange--even paradoxical--existence that we three have made for ourselves. In fact it is really too bad that you don´t believe in God. I´m an unbeliever myself, but I´ve always felt that for a woman. . .

FELICIA. -- Bull. If I were pious, you can be sure I would not have tolerated Irma´s presence in this household. I´d have left you long ago and I´d have returned to the country in Normandy.

ANATOLE. -- (Tenderly) Your religion, it´s me, isn´t it?

FELICIA. -- (In a dull-toned voice) I have no religion. Poor me.

ANATOLE. -- To live with an artist costs dearly; once again that´s certain. Especially these days. I was meant, you see, I myself was meant to live in another time and under more favorable circumstances. There is something in my nature that could only flourish in Venice or Florence, at the time of the Renaissance. A type like Michelangelo, who´s decried in foolish ways by imbeciles, fascinates me. He´s an idol of my dreams; I even find myself wondering--a poet´s thought that shouldn´t be treated lightly--if perhaps, who knows? in some previous life--

IRMA. -- (Entering at the height of her nervousness) You talk, you talk, and it´s ten minutes to three. In a few minutes, they´ll be here to pick us up.

FELICIA. -- What? How´s that?

ANATOLE. -- I haven´t yet had the chance to tell Felicia. (To Irma) Would you take care of that, my dear, while I get my coat.

IRMA. -- Charming. Thank you so much.

FELICIA. -- What is all this secretiveness about?

IRMA. -- No mystery, I assure you.

FELICIA. -- (In a peremptory tone) Toly, stay here.

IRMA. -- Something that in itself is insignificant but which might have considerable importance for his career. Anatole, it really seems to me that you shouldn´t leave me the care. . .

ANATOLE. -- I do my work. For the rest, I put myself. . .

IRMA. -- (In a persuasive tone) Felicia, you desire, don´t you, that his <u>Robespierre</u> be produced at the Odeon National Theater; you realize that Anatole will have a great opportunity--and that the Popular Front Government is entirely ready to require its director to present a work that glorifies a hero of the French Revolution.

FELICIA. -- Toly shouldn´t get involved in politics. Besides, the wind could change.

IRMA. -- Exactly, Felicia. As you say so well, the wind could change, so there is no time to lose. If the right regains power, Robespierre has had it. In this kind of a situation if an opportunity presents itself. . . Well, it´s just what has happened. Can you believe that the other day at a film, we met a childhood friend of mine. . .

FELICIA. -- You were at the movies together?

IRMA. -- That doesn´t matter.

FELICIA. -- What do you mean, that doesn´t matter? That´s against our ground rules.

IRMA. -- That friend whom I hadn´t seen in so long, but who recognized me right away, is the wife of a very influential member of Parliament who, it seems, has the ear of the Minister of Fine Arts.

FELICIA. -- At what movie?

IRMA. -- I don´t remember. We went to see a documentary film that wouldn´t have interested you, Felicia, I assure you.

FELICIA. -- (Dryly) Then what?

IRMA. -- That young woman. . . Well, she´s no longer really a young woman. . .

FELICIA. -- (Sarcastically) If she´s one of your childhood friends, I believe it.

IRMA. -- She and her husband have a lovely estate outside of Paris: Thirty acres, a stream a mile long; and they invited us to come for a weekend.

FELICIA. -- Who does that mean, us?

IRMA. -- But you understand. . .

FELICIA. -- Who does that mean, us?

IRMA. -- Anatole and me. You, in fact, they don´t even know you.

FELICIA. -- That does it; that´s the last straw.

IRMA. -- Anatole, I beg of you, explain.

ANATOLE. -- Not at all. You are doing it quite nicely.

IRMA. -- You know the noise and confusion in a movie theater. One can´t hear well. . . There was an incredible misunderstanding.

FELICIA. -- Which one?

IRMA. -- When I introduced Anatole, she thought I´d presented him as my husband.

ANATOLE. -- (Energetically) Besides, she is hard of hearing.

IRMA. -- You understand, Felicia. I said: "my friend" and she heard "my husband."

FELICIA. -- (Dryly) You didn´t have to say, "my friend."

IRMA. -- After that, naturally, I couldn´t explain matters, that would have been awkward. And the chauffeur is coming to pick us up in a few minutes.

FELICIA. -- (Exploding) Oh no! Irma, what do you think I am?

IRMA. -- But. . .

FELICIA. -- I ask, what do you take me for?

IRMA. -- For a superior woman, quite simply, Felicia. You are infinitely above small-minded pettiness.

FELICIA. -- Always the same tactic. You really should vary your approach.

IRMA. -- Moreover, when one has lived ten years in intimacy with an eminent man. . . As for myself, through his influence and yours, Felicia, yes, certainly, yours, I feel I have become a better person.

FELICIA. -- I'm sorry, but I haven't noticed anything of the sort. But enough! Nothing like a second misunderstanding to repair a first one. When the chauffeur arrives, I shall greet him. He'll think I'm the maid--it won't be the first time--and I'll tell him he was expected yesterday and that there is no one at home now.

IRMA. -- (In a tearful tone) You have no right to do that, Felicia. Think of Robespierre .

FELICIA. -- Robespierre and company. I assure you, my little friend, that at this moment I couldn't care less what becomes of them.

ANATOLE. -- (Pensively) There could perhaps be a solution. . . If it comes to it, I could go alone to the Foucard's.

IRMA. -- Anatole!

ANATOLE. -- (Indulgently) You could be ill, my dear friend. What am I saying? You are sick.

FELICIA. -- (Rudely) Certainly. And her neuralgia and her stomach aches.

ANATOLE. -- (Confidently) I think they will understand.

IRMA. -- (Acidly) You don't seem to realize that it's to me that you owe this invitation. If you had to rely solely on Felicia's good connections. . .

FELICIA. -- And do you think, by some stretch of the imagination, that you know my personal relations? I would never insult them by introducing them to you.

IRMA. -- Petit bourgeois who smell like mice. I can well imagine that.

FELICIA. -- Irma. Be careful.

IRMA. -- Me too, I've had enough.

FELICIA. -- Remember, you are in my house.

IRMA. -- The walls are yours.

FELICIA. -- And this table, it's not mine? And the eight chairs? And my grandmother's armchair.

IRMA. -- But the cupboard. . . and the chaise longue--

ANATOLE. -- (With a solemn condescension) I beg of you; I beg of you; don't you see that you are in the process of ruining a remarkable human achievement? My poor friends, it's as if you ravaged a work of art. You both are causing me untold pain. . . I was going to work; but my creative impulse has been shattered.

FELICIA. -- (To Irma) You see.

ANATOLE. -- It's the shipwreck of a great hope, that I

regret deeply. Hm! That´s quite poetic. Not my usual style, I admit. Note it nonetheless, Irma. You never know.

IRMA. -- I´m looking for a pencil and a paper. (Pause) And the car still hasn´t come.

ANATOLE. -- Now. Try to pull yourself together while I adjust my cravat. I don´t want to see a long face when I leave.

(He leaves.)

IRMA. -- Actually, he´d like nothing better than to go without me. And would you like to know why, Felicia?

FELICIA. -- I suppose I already know.

IRMA. -- After the cinema, we had a drink with Blanche Foucard. She practically threw herself at him. She´s the incandescent sort. Because of Robespierre , I let it pass, but I was furious. Well, if he goes there alone. . .

FELICIA. -- She has a husband.

IRMA. -- Don´t expect much from him. A politician of the arts, who they say has a preference for young boys. You understand, then, that she has a right to certain compensations too, and he can´t do anything more than look the other way. If I don´t go you can imagine how this scenario will end. Now, if you don´t care.

FELICIA. -- Even admitting. . . It´s not because you prevent them from sleeping together this time. . .

IRMA. -- (With feeling) I beg your pardon. She must realize he´s someone else´s. I´ll let Blanche know that she has me to contend with.

FELICIA. -- (Bitterly) Finally, what does it matter to me whether he sleeps with this one or with someone else?

IRMA. -- That´s what you say, Felicia. But before I moved in here, your life was a living hell. I´ve forgotten nothing of what you told me. When he didn´t come in until mornings, and in what shape then! When he brought home ladies of the night. . . And his flight into Belgium. When you suggested that I come here, you had your reasons. You know he would have left you for good.

FELICIA. -- Maybe that would have been better. . . What do I know?

IRMA. -- That´s just talk, Felicia. He´s settled down, he´s working regularly.

FELICIA. -- (Softly, with hate) Yes, but you, your presence. . . Haven´t you realized yet that I hate you?

(A silence. The door bell rings.)

IRMA. -- There´s the bell; I´ll answer it.

FELICIA. -- No, I´ll go.

IRMA. -- Felicia. Don´t make a scene. Think of Anatole.

(Felicia remains still.)

(Aimee sticking her head through the door at the right.)

AIMEE. -- Mother. Someone´s at the door.

IRMA. -- Would you be good enough to answer the door, Aimee ?

(Aimee leaves.)

FELICIA. -- You are trying to force my hand.

IRMA. -- I tell you again, she is a dangerous woman.

FELICIA. -- By the way, what kind of an explanation of all this are you going to give to your daughter?

IRMA. -- Oh. Any one at all. Aimee is not a complicated child.

FELICIA. -- I´m beginning to see that.

(Aimee coming in.)

AIMEE.-- It´s a lady and gentlemen who are asking for Mr. and Mrs. Girondin. (She hands a calling card to Felicia.)

FELICIA. -- Mr. and Mrs. Lucien Foucard.

IRMA. -- They came themselves. (To Aimee) Show them in.

FELICIA. -- Let´s see this ardent lady.

(Outlandish contrast between the people and the description Irma had given of them. Blanche is austerity itself; the couple exude an air of correct boredom.)

IRMA. -- It´s so gracious of you! Anatole is coming right away, I just have to get my hat. . .

BLANCHE. -- There´s no need to rush, dear Madam. We´re not in any hurry.

IRMA. -- (Speaking offstage) Anatole, Mr. and Mrs. Foucard are here.

ANATOLE. -- (From outside) I´m coming.

IRMA. -- Would you like something to eat or drink?

FOUCARD. -- (With a cavernous voice) Thank you, no. I never take anything between meals.

BLANCHE. -- Besides we´ve just finished eating. A corporation banquet that my husband was asked to preside.

IRMA. -- (In a half whisper to Felicia, who has slumped into an armchair. Only her back can be seen shaken by convulsive sobs.) Felicia, please.

FELICIA. -- You didn´t even introduce me.

IRMA. -- Well what am I thinking of! May I introduce Mrs. Rosary, a relative who unfortunately isn´t well at all.

(Compassionate murmurs from the Foucards) She has painful neuralgia that has made a veritable martyr of her. . . Excuse me a minute.

(She exits.)

AIMEE. -- (Stupified) How´s that! But, my cousin. . .
BLANCHE. -- I pity you, Madam. Isn´t there any tranquilizer for that sort of pain?
FOUCARD. -- Medicine still has a long way to go.
BLANCHE. -- We often say, my husband and I: "The science of medicine is still in its childhood."
FOUCARD. -- However, by contrast, surgery. . .
BLANCHE. -- My husband is correct; sometimes surgery works miracles.

(A silence)

AIMEE. -- But, my cousin, this came on you so quickly. At noon you weren´t sick at all.
FOUCARD. -- Always these damn neuralgias.

(Irma reappears, dressed to go out, her hat on her head. Anatole follows her.)

IRMA. -- Poor Felicia. It´s dreadful to have to leave you in such a state. I´m almost wondering if perhaps we shouldn´t. . .
ANATOLE. -- The aspirin hasn´t had time enough to work yet.
BLANCHE. -- It is true that it never works right away.
ANATOLE. -- (Indicating Aimee) Besides she´s in good hands.
BLANCHE. -- That´s true. I´m sure Aimee will do her very best.
AIMEE. -- Oh! Yes, Mother.
ANATOLE. -- We would only tire her. . . I believe it´s better for her. . .
BLANCHE. -- Exactly. I know when I have migraines. . .
FOUCARD. -- Come, come, we´re tiring Madam. . .
ANATOLE. -- Poor dear. . . (Sniffling by Irma.)
IRMA. -- (To Aimee) Bye-bye, my little sweetheart. We´ll see you tomorrow night.
ANATOLE. -- The overnight bag is in the vestibule.

(They leave)

(A silence)

FELICIA. -- (Turning toward Aimee) Run downstairs after your Mother. Tell her that I´m going to explain everything to you. Do you understand, I am going to give you a full and complete explanation. . . No, instead, just simply say: Mother, Cousin Felicia said to tell you that she will dot the i´s. Do you understand?

AIMEE. -- (Timidly) But, cousin. . .

FELICIA. -- Hurry, go along.

(Aimee leaves. Felicia, left alone, goes to the window, opens it, leans out, and in an impulsive gesture closes the shutters. The room is plunged into darkness. Felicia goes to the wall switch and turns the electric light on. Aimee returns moments later; she waits at the threshold, bewildered.)

AIMEE. -- What´s this? It´s still full daylight. Why did you turn the lights on, cousin?

FELICIA. -- Because I wanted to. Did you do what I asked?

AIMEE. -- (In a hesitant tone.) Yes. . .

FELICIA. -- Exactly as I told you?

AIMEE. -- Well, I didn´t say that part, you know, about dotting the i´s. That would have sounded strange.

FELICIA. -- (Coldly) To whom?

AIMEE. -- Well. . . to that gentleman and that lady who don´t know you. . .

FELICIA. -- And you, Aimee, do you imagine that you by chance know me?

AIMEE. -- Oh! No, cousin.

FELICIA. -- Stop constantly saying cousin, cousin, cousin. It drives me crazy.

AIMEE. -- As you say, cou. . . Do you still have your headache?

FELICIA. -- No. It´s gone.

AIMEE. -- Oh! That´s good. They must be very painful.

FELICIA. -- Look at me, Aimee. Didn´t you notice anything?

AIMEE. -- Notice? Notice what?

FELICIA. -- Do you really believe an attack came on me like that from one minute to the next?

AIMEE. -- I don´t know. I just believe what I´m told. Why do you speak to me in such a harsh tone? I haven´t hurt you, cousin. Or at least I didn´t mean to, I assure you.

FELICIA. -- (In a softer tone) Of course not, I have nothing to reproach you for.

AIMEE. -- Oh! I think you are probably not very happy to have me in your home.

FELICIA. -- Where did you get that idea?

(A vague gesture from Aimee.)

AIMEE. -- But you do know it´s not my fault. I didn´t want to come to Paris.

FELICIA. -- You didn´t want to?

AIMEE. -- Oh! (With obvious insincerity) Naturally I was happy to see Mother.

FELICIA. -- Ah! Yes. . . And Paris? You didn´t want to see something of the world?

AIMEE. -- No, not really. It´s rare, you know, that I really want something.

FELICIA. -- At your age!

AIMEE. -- Well, actually, yes, I would like to be at home.

FELICIA. -- At your Father´s home in the South, weren´t you content?

AIMEE. -- Oh! No, you see. . . I was in the way. . .

FELICIA. -- Your foster mother, she wasn´t good to you?

AIMEE. -- (Frightened) Who ever said that?

FELICIA. -- I´m asking you.

AIMEE. -- Mother Simone wasn´t mean. But she too, she had troubles. Stomach. So often she was upset. Besides that, it can´t be helped, but I think I got on her nerves. It wasn´t her fault.

FELICIA. -- It´s since the birth of your little brother that she has pains in her stomach?

AIMEE. -- Yes, I think so. It´s terrible, don´t you think? How there are so many people who have suffering, illnesses, and pain. One wonders why.

FELICIA. -- (With bitterness) Yes, one wonders why.

AIMEE. -- But it seems we shouldn´t; that´s what Father Flower said.

FELICIA. -- Father who?

AIMEE. -- (With simplicity) Father Flower.

FELICIA. -- What a strange name for a priest.

AIMEE. --You think so? I´m used to it. It was with him that I prepared for my first communion. I´m speaking of my solemn communion at the time of my confirmation.

FELICIA. -- Do you often think of your first communion?

AIMEE. -- Oh! yes, I just have to think of it sometimes.

FELICIA. -- (in a different tone) You should go outside, and get some fresh air, Aimee. Otherwise you won´t have any appetite for dinner.

AIMEE. -- (In a pleading tone.) I really don´t feel like a walk, cousin.

FELICIA. -- (Dryly) Well, I certainly don´t plan to go for a walk with you.

AIMEE. -- Oh! But I never would have thought.

FELICIA. -- All you have to do is turn right; in two minutes you´re on the boulevard. . . There are nice shops there; you can look at the window displays. You don´t have to be afraid; no one will say anything to you.

AIMEE. -- I don´t particularly like to look at shop displays. Except for toy shops.

FELICIA. -- (Astonished) Toys? At your age?

AIMEE. -- Oh! It´s not for me, as you might think. It´s for baby Jim.

FELICIA. -- How old is he, your little brother?

AIMEE. -- He´ll be four years old, the sixth of next month. Have I showed you his photo?

FELICIA. -- No.

AIMEE-- I´ll go get it.

(She goes out. A silence. Felicia is nervous. She taps with her fingers on the table. Aimee comes back after a moment.)

AIMEE. -- Look, see. He´s beautiful! And his curls. They´re like gold.

FELICIA. -- You love your baby brother a great deal, don´t you?

AIMEE. -- (In a sort of sob) Oh! yes. . . (With despair) Cousin, do you think that I could go and see him sometimes? Otherwise. . . he´ll forget me. . . He´ll forget me. . . at four, just think. . .!

FELICIA. -- Of course not. He won´t forget you. . . And then you father will send for you, don´t you think?

AIMEE. -- Traveling costs a lot of money.

FELICIA. -- Anatole has a relative who works for the railroad. Maybe he could get you a ticket half price.

AIMEE. -- Even so. . . Who will pay for it?

FELICIA. -- Don´t worry about that.

(A silence.)

AIMEE. -- (Pursuing her own thought.) It´s strange that when I was born they had the idea of naming me "Aimee," from the French "Aimee" meaning the loved one. Don´t you think so?

FELICIA. -- I have the impression you spend a lot of time worrying. You shouldn´t, you know.

AIMEE. -- Can one make oneself not worry?

FELICIA. -- Try a little to be more like your mother. She´s one who always takes life by its good side.

AIMEE. -- That´s bad?

FELICIA. -- I suppose that it´s lucky.

AIMEE. -- Does cousin Anatole too?

FELICIA. -- He´s an artist.

AIMEE. -- And Mother?

FELICIA. -- (Harshly) Ah! No.

AIMEE. -- Cousin, tell me. . . No, pardon. . . Well, what exactly does it mean to "Dot the i´s?"

FELICIA. -- Oh! It´s a cliché.

AIMEE. -- That doesn´t mean anything?

FELICIA. -- Not much.

AIMEE. -- Then why did you tell me to say it to Mother?

(A silence)

AIMEE. -- You promised that you would give me a full explanation.

FELICIA. -- Of what?

AIMEE. -- But first of all, that gentleman and that lady. Mother told them your name was Mrs. Rosary. . . or did I misunderstand?

FELICIA. -- I wasn´t really listening at that point.

AIMEE. -- I must not have heard her correctly. I sometimes do that. Mother Simone thinks I´ll be deaf later on.

FELICIA. -- What does she know about it?

AIMEE-- I wouldn´t like to be deaf. One must feel so alone. It would be worse than being blind, don´t you think? Oh! Cousin, do you think they´ll find a situation "au pair" where I can live and work with a family? And, what will I have to do?

FELICIA. -- Well I don´t know, Aimee. Maybe take care of children.

AIMEE. -- (With enthusiasm) I´d really like that. . . Wouldn´t you have liked to have children, cousin?

FELICIA. -- (In a low tone) Well, you know, dear, it isn´t just a question of choice.

AIMEE. -- Well, some of Madame Simone´s friends say they don´t want any children, and they don´t have any; so it must be able to be arranged. In any case, if I marry. . .

FELICIA. -- Well?

AIMEE. -- I´d like to have children right away. Twins, a boy and a girl. It would be wonderful to raise them together, a lovely little pair.

FELICIA. -- (Painfully) Aimee, I once had twins, a long time ago; one was dead at birth, the other lived two days.

AIMEE. -- (Astounded) My cousin!

FELICIA. -- And since then. . . doctors have told me that I can´t have any more children. Not ever. Or I would die in childbirth.

AIMEE. -- But your twins are angels in heaven.

FELICIA. -- Do you believe there are angels, Aimee?

AIMEE. -- Father Flower speaks of them often.

FELICIA. -- What does he know about them, this Father Flower, now I ask you?

AIMEE. -- You shouldn´t talk like that, cousin, that´s a sin. (Gravely) Once the Church teaches something, one must believe it. You have a guardian angel, you know.

FELICIA. -- And your Mother, she has a guardian angel too?

AIMEE. -- Certainly, everyone does.

FELICIA. -- And what do they do all together, these guardian angels? Do they quarrel?

AIMEE. -- (Scandalized) Cousin. You shouldn´t joke like that. That´s a sin too.

FELICIA. -- You are really up on all that.

AIMEE. -- (Timidly) You don´t go to confession?

FELICIA. -- Never.

AIMEE. -- That must be terrible.

FELICIA. -- Not at all.

AIMEE. -- Oh! Yes . . . I, I would just die.

FELICIA. -- What are you talking about?

AIMEE. -- If I couldn´t confess, I´d die. It would be as if. . . as if I could no longer breathe. If one can no longer breathe, one dies, that´s the way it is. But there it´s not the body, it´s the soul that dies. However, the soul doesn´t die since it´s immortal. . .

FELICIA. -- You see, you´re getting it all mixed up.

AIMEE. -- I´m going to tell you a secret, cousin. When Papa told me that he had to get an apartment that wouldn´t have enough room for me. . . when I understood that I could no longer take care of my little brother, that I would no longer see him for a long time, that gave me an awful shock . . . I suddenly thought, if Mother Simone were no longer there, it would be I who would raise James, I would be his little Mother. . . Well, I couldn´t help but wish she wouldn´t get better; do you understand? I almost. . . prayed that she would die. . . But after that I was so ashamed, I no longer dared look at her. . . I didn´t dare go to confession. I was miserable! Then one day I met the priest. . . He saw something in my eyes. He spoke so gently to me. That was still nothing; but it gave me the courage to go to him for confession. And those thoughts left me, I felt light, happy.

FELICIA. -- (In a muffled voice) You know, Aimee, it´s not always bad to wish someone´s death.

AIMEE. -- Oh! Cousin, how can you say that? But first there are people, you know, who think that a thought is something real. . . like a weapon that can hurt somebody, that can. . .

FELICIA. -- In any event, it´s not to me that you should be telling these stories. (With increasing passion) I, you must realize, Aimee, I have nothing to reproach myself for. Absolutely nothing. If they knew everything, perhaps they´d even find. . . There are not many who in my place would have had the courage. . . because, it was courage. I did what was best, you hear. . . At least, I believed. (She bursts into tears.) It´s the others. . . Oh! those others!

AIMEE. -- What others?

FELICIA. -- (Without answering) If I´d only had a child like you. . . simply like you. . . I didn´t ask for anything extraordinary. . . The little bit I had, I wanted to keep. The little bit I had. . .

AIMEE. -- Those who have hurt you, cousin, are they--?

(Felicia shakes her head as if to convey that she cannot answer.)

AIMEE. -- That is not my business?

(Again Felicia shakes her head.)

AIMEE. -- I shall never know?

(Another shaking of Felicia´s head.)

AIMEE. -- I have perhaps guessed, you know.
FELICIA. -- No.
AIMEE. -- You don´t want me to guess?
FELICIA. -- I don´t want it, I don´t want it anymore.
AIMEE. -- You´re crying now like a child. . . like a little child, my cousin.

(She drops to her knees; she puts her arms around Felicia´s neck.)

Paris, November 6-9, 1936
Gabriel Marcel

THE DOUBLE EXPERTISE

A Comedy In One Act

by

Gabriel Marcel

Translated by Katharine Rose Hanley

CAST OF CHARACTERS

(in order of appearance)

GILBERT MARQUISET	Husband-to-be for a third time
GEORGETTE	First wife of Gilbert; second wife of Stani
STANI	Second husband to Georgette; estranged son of the appraiser
KATE LELIEGEOIS	Second wife of Gilbert; claiming alimony
HEDWIG FRUHLING	Third bride-to-be of Gilbert; pays prospective visit to Gilbert´s apartment chaperoned properly by an appraiser
MR. ZURCHER	The appraiser; chaperon for Hedwig Fruhling

Paris 1937

THE DOUBLE EXPERTISE
A One Act Comedy by Gabriel Marcel

An elegant bachelor´s apartment
Scene I
Gilbert, Stani, Georgette

GEORGETTE, -- There! You see how prompt we are, Gilbert darling. Marvelous, isn´t it? And we came by subway. It was I who insisted upon that. Hm? What do you say to that? I who was always late, do you remember? I who wasted my money on taxis?

GILBERT. -- Your money. . . oh well, you spent it. . .

GEORGETTE. -- Remember our marriage contract. We had common funds, a joint account, Gil darling.

GILBERT. -- Stani really is someone very special. But his feigned air of modesty doesn´t fool me; he knows his worth.

GEORGETTE. -- Gil darling, you won´t believe this, but in fact, it´s you who taught me to be economical.

GILBERT. -- Too bad the fruit of my efforts came so late. Especially since you, for your part, you turned me into a spendthrift.

GEORGETTE. -- In our times, you were rather tight.

GILBERT. -- We´ve both changed.

STANI. -- While, as for me, I haven´t budged.

GEORGETTE. -- What´s more, you´re a homesticker, Stani. It´s the same thing with summer villas too. (To Gilbert) Last summer, we´d reserved rooms in a certain hotel in Chamonix which, upon arrival, we found to be terrible. Well, Stani wouldn´t hear of looking for another place. So, as a result, I had an upset stomach. Still, everything taken into account, I have to admit life is more restful. Do you remember, Gil, we couldn´t stay put? The day after our arrival, you´d say, "Let´s ask for the bill." And we´d be off.

GILBERT. -- That had its charm.

GEORGETTE. -- You´ll have to become a convert to monotony . . . and to green vegetables.

GILBERT. -- That will be difficult. Stani, have you nothing to say?

STANI. -- I´m listening to you with interest. You speak of your life together as if it were a picnic. . . and not too successful a one at that.

GEORGETTE. -- But we do, after all, have happy memories, don´t we, Gil?

GILBERT. -- Quite.

GEORGETTE. -- That´s sweet.

GILBERT. -- Overall.

STANI. -- Let us hope that if in the future we meet, let us say, me facing my successor, like Gilbert and you. . .

GEORGETTE. -- What do you mean, your successor? How can you say that, Stani? It´s practically a lack of tact. We´re just like people who bought an apartment.

STANI. -- You can resell an apartment, you know.

GEORGETTE. -- But at a loss, so one stays there.

STANI. -- That´s reassuring.

GEORGETTE. -- But now it´s time for Gilbert to settle down too. That´s why I can´t wait to meet this young lady. You haven´t described her to me at all, Gil.

GILBERT. -- Descriptions aren´t my forte.

GEORGETTE. -- Is she big or little?

GILBERT. -- We´re not playing guessing games; you´ll see her in a few minutes.

GEORGETTE. -- Does she please you?

GILBERT. -- In fact she´s very attractive. But her appearance varies from day to day. Day before yesterday, she really looked a mess.

GEORGETTE. -- That´s annoying. Don´t you think so, Stani?

GILBERT. -- Perhaps her dress just didn´t suit her.

GEORGETTE. -- If she doesn´t know how to dress. . . (To Stani) Gilbert´s odd that way, he appears very observant without actually being so.

STANI. -- That is curious.

GEORGETTE. -- He has definite impressions, but without being able to explain them.

GILBERT. -- It´s really good of you to be willing to offer me your opinion.

STANI. -- An expert opinion like any other. (Said modestly)

GILBERT. -- Georgette knows my tastes and habits so well.

GEORGETTE. -- But now I never make a decision without consulting Stani; he accompanies me to all my fittings. That´s why I wanted to bring him here.

GILBERT. -- How fortunate that he was free!

STANI. -- Forced leisure, I´m afraid.

GILBERT. -- Business not so good?

STANI. -- You said it!

GEORGETTE. -- "You said it" hardly has a plural reference.

STANI. -- What are you talking about?

GEORGETTE. -- It´s just a slight nuance. But Gil is a purist, you see. (To Gilbert) Were you able to get exact information about her financial situation? That is important, you know.

GILBERT. -- I know it only too well. . .

GEORGETTE. -- It´s capital. You can´t afford a blunder.

GILBERT. -- That´s my opinion exactly.

GEORGETTE. -- This time you mustn´t go against your innermost feelings. That´s too dangerous, my dear little Gil.

GILBERT. -- Her father owns three big hotels.

STANI. -- Tourism is declining, don´t forget that.

GILBERT. -- In Switzerland?

STANI. -- Well, that´s a different matter. Switzerland is holding its own pretty well. But try and get some prospectus on the hotels. I´ll look them over carefully.

GILBERT. -- It´s a bit awkward to ask for them, you know.

STANI. -- Not at all. Make up some excuse. Friends who are looking for a summer resort. Or whatever comes to mind.

GEORGETTE. -- Stani´s right. . . This young lady is alone in Paris?

GILBERT. -- If I understand rightly, she´s living with an aunt.

GEORGETTE. -- She doesn´t seem too emancipated, does she? Actually I think you need a sort of old-fashioned girl.

GILBERT. -- I´m not an old fogy.

GEORGETTE. -- You are so easily shocked, Gil; I´ve always noticed that. It´s a charming trait for a man, one that´s all too rare.

STANI. -- (Grumbling) On the other hand, one shouldn´t be prudish either.

GEORGETTE. -- In the beginning, Stani used to say some pretty gross things with his friend Gus. But he´s getting over that. Still, to get back to that young lady. I´m a bit uneasy, my dear little Gilbert. You don´t even know if she suits you.

GILBERT. -- I know, every time I try to make a decision, my mind muddles.

GEORGETTE. -- That´s really too bad. What´s more, there´s that nasty precedent.

GILBERT. -- I can see that you´re constantly thinking of Kate. . .

GEORGETTE. -- You were lucky to get out of that one alive, Gil dear. I´ve often said it to Stani, you really flirted with danger that time, really courted disaster.

GILBERT. -- Let´s not exaggerate.

GEORGETTE. -- But that´s exactly what makes me feel better. Stani´s half-brother, who´s really very clever, Doctor Zurcher-Salomon, says that everyone has to have one major sickness in life. The same thing holds true for our feelings. You know, I always considered your marriage with Kate to be merely a parenthetical break.

GILBERT. -- If I´d only known. . .

GEORGETTE.-- You wouldn´t have listened, Gil dear. At that time, we exchanged some pretty cutting remarks. I can´t remember exactly what they were. I have no memory for that sort of thing. Still, you understand, had I told you at that time what I thought of Kate, you would have thought it was because of bitterness. . .Well, perhaps.

GILBERT. -- Fortunately, we can say everything worked out fine.

GEORGETTE.-- For the best, Gil dear, if you ask me. . . Is she in Paris?

GILBERT. -- Who? Kate? I don´t know. She doesn´t have a telephone anymore. I don´t want to write. And I can´t very well ask her doorman for progress reports.

GEORGETTE.-- Of course not. But I´m amazed that she no longer has a telephone. That´s how she spent most of her time.

GILBERT.-- I think she´s about flat broke.

GEORGETTE. -- But, don´t you pay her alimony?

GILBERT.-- Theoretically, yes. But, I myself am rather short for the moment.

GEORGETTE. -- You should have told us sooner. It´s true that Stani too is. . .

STANI. -- Financially embarrassed.

GEORGETTE. -- These times are awful. Don´t you think so, Gil?

GILBERT. -- Disgusting.

STANI. -- What time is she supposed to come? And while we´re at it, what´s her name?

GILBERT. -- Hedwig. Hedwig Fruhling.

STANI. -- Hmm! A strange name. A bit démodé. Don´t you think?

GEORGETTE. -- So much the better. Don´t you think it´s a bit odd that she accepted a rendezvous at your apartment?

GILBERT. -- Oh no! She´ll be accompanied.

GEORGETTE. -- Oh! By her aunt?

GILBERT. -- No. Her aunt is an invalid.

GEORGETTE. -- Then the girl is a practical nurse?

GILBERT. -- I don´t think so.

GEORGETTE. -- (To Stani) It wouldn´t be so bad for Gil to marry a nurse.

GILBERT. -- How awful! . . .

GEORGETTE. -- You know, Gil, in certain circumstances, it´s a great advantage. Nowadays nurses are so expensive, you have no idea how much they cost.

STANI. -- There´s the bell.

GEORGETTE. -- Will someone let her in?

GILBERT. -- Yes. The doorman´s daughter.

(A silence.)

SCENE II

Gilbert, Georgette, Stani, Kate

KATE. -- (Stopping on the threshold) Well.

GILBERT. -- (Very embarrassed) We were just talking about you, just a moment ago, Madame.

KATE. -- You address me formally now?

GILBERT. -- You know. . .Madame Leliegeois. . .Monsieur et Madame Zurcher.

GEORGETTE. -- These amenities are entirely superfluous.

(A silence. Kate sits.)

KATE. -- What´s the matter with you? You´re green.

GILBERT. -- Come now!

GEORGETTE. -- Gilbert never did have very good color.

KATE. -- When I knew him he was rather congested.

GEORGETTE. -- After meals.

KATE. -- Not only then. Although he ate too much.

GEORGETTE. -- You astound me.

KATE.-- I know what I´m talking about. (Eyeing a painting) What´s that I see? A Dufy? You are living in high style.

GILBERT. -- (Excitedly) It´s a present.

KATE. -- That, my friend, is worth at least two thousand.

GILBERT. -- I have no idea about that.

KATE. -- I´ve got a taker.

GILBERT. -- You´re dreaming! I´ve no intention of parting with that. . .

KATE. -- That makes no difference to me! All I care is that I get the thousand I need.

GILBERT. -- You are unbelievable.

GEORGETTE. -- It seems, to my husband and to me. . .

KATE. -- I beg your pardon? You can take it down, your Dufy. I´ll take it with me.

GILBERT. -- Then, you´re seizing it?

KATE. -- Reclaiming it.

GEORGETTE. -- (In a half whisper) The parenthesis has claws and a beak.

STANI. -- If you please, Madame, I have not completely forgotten my training in law. . .

KATE. -- I warn you that I´m unbeatable.

GEORGETTE. -- (To Stani) If I were you, I wouldn´t hazard a contest on this topic. . . My dear Madame, Gilbert, at one time, could have given me an ultimatum on similar accounts. I must say he was generous. . .

KATE. -- The idiot. And at my expense. I´ve criticized him enough for it. . .Besides, how do I know that you don´t pay him alimony?

STANI. -- I assure you. . .

KATE. -- (To Gilbert) What do you live on, I can´t help but wonder?

GEORGETTE. -- That´s despicable. We´ll hear no more of it.

(She rises.)

GILBERT. -- Georgette, I beg you. . .remember. . .

GEORGETTE. -- (To Stani, sharply) Stani, let me tell you that you are the lowest of the low. Gilbert is in an impossible situation. . .

STANI. -- And my situation, don´t you find it a bit "gauche"?

GEORGETTE. -- I hate it when you throw in those French phrases. You can hear your German accent, and that makes you sound more Yiddish than usual.

GILBERT. -- (To Kate) I´m telling you again. I´m waiting for my dividend payment.

GEORGETTE. -- (To Kate) Dear Madame, would you be kind enough to listen to me?

KATE. -- Why don´t you get your tonsils removed? That would do you good, you know.

GEORGETTE. -- In just a few minutes a meeting will occur here, a moving encounter that could have most fortunate consequences. Gilbert has recently become acquainted with a lovely young woman. . .She´s Swiss.

KATE. -- Oh! My. . .It sounds like a Nestle´s commercial. . .But I must admit change is wonderful.

GEORGETTE. -- Obviously, it´s not desirable that this meeting take place in the presence of a third party.

KATE. -- Very well. Let´s leave him alone. Are you coming?

GILBERT. -- I asked Georgette and Stani to assist me.

KATE. -- That´s tough; and me?

GILBERT. -- I didn´t even know you were in Paris.

KATE. -- And why shouldn´t I also have the right to vote?

GILBERT. -- That would seem too much like a jury.

KATE. -- I´m staying. And what´s more, I´m not leaving without some security.

GILBERT. -- (To Georgette, in a whisper) That´s a catastrophe.

STANI. -- Madame, may I point out that you risk becoming the first victim of this inappropriate behavior.

KATE. -- (Half audibly) Shit!

GEORGETTE. -- What did she say? (The doorbell rings.) I am excited, you know, Gil dear.

Scene III

Gilbert, Georgette, Stani, Kate, Hedwig, Monsieur Zurcher

GILBERT. -- (Going to greet the new arrivals.) Dear Mademoiselle, I am so happy. . .(He stops, shocked to see Monsieur Zurcher.)

HEDWIG. -- Monsieur Zurcher is a good friend of my aunt´s.

STANI. -- (To Georgette) Father! That´s fantastic!

GEORGETTE. -- Stani, please, calm yourself. . .

GILBERT. -- Let me present. . .my cousin Stanislas, my cousin Georgette, Mademoiselle Fruhling.

MR. ZURCHER. -- Cousins?

STANI. -- (Dryly) On my wife´s side.

GILBERT. -- Kate Leliegeois--a distant relative.

KATE. -- How´s that, distant?

HEDWIG. -- We´re quite tired. Monsieur Zurcher made me visit three exhibits. . .It was extremely interesting, but also extremely tiring.

GEORGETTE. -- Do you like painting?

HEDWIG. -- Not too much. Especially modern painting. You can´t recognize anything.

MR. ZURCHER. -- And I who showed you only abstract art.

HEDWIG. -- One must recognize.

GILBERT. -- Mademoiselle Fruhling loves nature passionately.

GEORGETTE. -- We too love nature avidly, don´t we, Stani?

KATE. -- Nature bores me.

HEDWIG. -- How´s that, Madame?

KATE. -- (Aggressively) Especially mountains.

GEORGETTE. -- Tsk! Tsk!

KATE. -- I can´t climb because of my asthma, and below it´s suffocating.

HEDWIG. -- (Indulgently) Naturally, if you are sick--But one can always go to resorts in the high Alps. There are panoramic views one never tires of, for example, at Montana, at Rigi. . .It´s magnificent. The sunrises are something . . .

GEORGETTE. -- It does one good to see someone so admiring. It´s refreshing, isn´t it, Stani?

STANI. -- (Inarticulate) Hum, hum!

HEDWIG. -- Every year in June, when I see the Alpine mountain flowers, the alpine roses, the edelweiss, the anemones. I exclaim aloud, I even feel like crying.

GEORGETTE. -- Isn´t that charming.

KATE. -- You must not be at home in Paris, Mademoiselle...

HEDWIG. -- It´s entirely different, naturally.

KATE. -- Quite.

GEORGETTE. -- Would you like to live there?

HEDWIG. -- All cities are dreadful, but one must live there nonetheless. One must resign oneself. Fortunately weekends one can go on excursions into the countryside.

GEORGETTE. -- By car?

HEDWIG. -- Oh no, on foot, along secluded country paths. At the end of the day, one is tired.

GILBERT. -- Very tired.

HEDWIG. -- Not very tired; just a little tired. It´s very healthy; one is hungry, and one sleeps well.

GILBERT. -- I´m afraid of just the opposite--that I wouldn´t sleep a wink.

HEDWIG. -- You don´t get enough exercise; that will have to change.

KATE. -- Gilbert has found his master.

HEDWIG. -- At home, it´s I who am the doctor.

GEORGETTE. -- She is a sketch.

STANI. -- Are you studying medicine, Mademoiselle?

HEDWIG. -- I know all about plants.

GILBERT. -- Mademoiselle is a naturalist.

KATE. -- To the point of nudism, included?

HEDWIG. -- (Dryly) Madame. What´s that you said?

GEORGETTE. -- Nature certainly accomplishes miracles.

STANI. -- I wouldn´t count on it.

HEDWIG. -- Uncle Ed knows something about it. Isn´t it true that I cured your migraines, Uncle Ed?

MR. ZURCHER. -- One might say that.

HEDWIG. -- You shouldn´t say: "one might say"; you should say, "of course." "One might say" sounds so negative.

GEORGETTE. -- How´s that?

MR. ZURCHER. -- Mademoiselle Fruhling is a member of the <u>Renovation Group.</u>

HEDWIG. -- You too, Uncle Ed!

MR. ZURCHER. -- Up to a point.

HEDWIG. -- No, no, no, no, no. . .

STANI. -- The migraines vanished and you were converted?

HEDWIG. -- (To Georgette) You husband uses such a familiar tone with Uncle Ed?

GEORGETTE. -- He´s his son. . .

HEDWIG. -- Uncle Ed, this man is your son?

MR. ZURCHER. -- In fact, yes.

HEDWIG. -- And you concealed this fact?

GILBERT. -- I´ll go out and get some cool drinks!

HEDWIG. -- Uncle Ed, you concealed your son.

GEORGETTE. -- My husband and his father have had a serious disagreement. . .

HEDWIG. -- I know now why I had the inspiration to bring Uncle Ed here with me.

KATE. -- Inspiration? What does that mean?

HEDWIG. -- Uncle Ed, explain, please?

MR. ZURCHER. -- It´s a bit difficult for me.

HEDWIG. -- It´s not difficult at all. It´s only a question of not being afraid to profess one´s belief.

MR. ZURCHER. -- My child, I´ve already told you. . .

HEDWIG. -- During this morning´s meditation it came to me. Uncle Ed will come with me to Gilbert Marquiset´s. Later we´ll go out on the porch, we´ll enjoy the view and you can settle things with your son.

STANI. -- Settle things?

GEORGETTE. -- But it was precisely over the settlement of my mother-in-law´s estate that their disagreement began.

HEDWIG. -- (Disdainfully) I´m not talking about that kind of settlement.

KATE. -- (To Gilbert) She´s crazy, your Dulcinea.

GILBERT. -- Dear Mademoiselle, don´t you think it´s a bit risky to get involved in the affairs of others?

HEDWIG. -- Because I received the inspiration, I must do something.

GILBERT. -- Wouldn´t it be more discreet...?

(Kate ostentatiously lets herself go into a fit of giddy laughter.)

HEDWIG. -- Discretion is a cover for egotism, and cowardice. Professor Spielbaum explained that at Ragatz´s house party. . .That woman´s laughter is forced. She´s not happy, she´s a bit hysterical.

KATE. -- Mind your own business, hm!. . .

GEORGETTE. -- (To Gilbert in a half whisper) Now tell me, Gil dear, what is the meaning of this savage?

GILBERT. -- I´ve never seen her carry on like this. It´s frightful.

GEORGETTE. -- Naturally, it´s too early to say, but I can´t help but wonder. . .

GILBERT. -- (Exasperated. To Mr. Zurcher who is examining and evaluating furnishings as if he were a commissioned appraiser.) This is not an auction hall, if you please.

MR. ZURCHER. -- (Unperturbed) I promised an old friend that I´d appraise. . .

GILBERT. -- Oh. Then you are here as an appraiser?

MR. ZURCHER. -- Call it what you will.

GILBERT. -- (Exasperated) That´s just great.

MR. ZURCHER. -- (To Hedwig) My dear, make of it what you will, but nothing of what I see here gives me the least bit of confidence.

GEORGETTE. -- What nerve! It was I who bought all this for him at the finest antique shops!

MR. ZURCHER. -- But, Madame. How can I know that you weren´t working for a commission. . .

GEORGETTE. -- (Stridently) Stani! Your father´s insulting me!

STANI. -- You don´t want me to strangle the old man, do you?

GEORGETTE. -- You never had any family feelings before; now is no time to start.

HEDWIG. -- (To Gilbert) Your cousins are really strange people. . . What´s more, one doesn´t address one´s daughter-in-law as Madame. I´ve never encountered anything like this.

MR. ZURCHER. -- (Pointing to a miniature) Just a moment, my dear man. Take this, for example, you´re not going to try and tell me that it´s genuine.

GILBERT. -- That one I´ll concede. I´ve been trying to unload it for a long time.

KATE. -- (Shrilly) Ungrateful slob! I gave that to you our last night together, after our farewell dinner.

HEDWIG. -- What?

KATE. -- Exactly. This fine man was my husband for fourteen months, if you want to know. . .And before that, this little snipe was his wife for two and a half years.

GEORGETTE. -- Three years less one day.

(Gilbert has dropped into an armchair; he seems devastated.)

MR. ZURCHER. -- My dear, I think we have no further business here.

HEDWIG. -- (Looking at Gil pitifully) I understand why you look so tired. . .There´s reason to be.

(Gil sighs.)

KATE. -- (Sharply) You should nevertheless know. . .

HEDWIG. -- I´m the doctor. Either we stay and behave as a group--that means that one remains quiet and listens to one´s conscience--or you others leave and I shall stay with Gilbert.

GEORGETTE. -- But, Mademoiselle, I´m astonished. . .

KATE. -- Well listen to that. What cheek. However, again I repeat, I´m not leaving here without some stake.

HEDWIG. -- A stake? Are you playing a game? You can finish that later on.

MR. ZURCHER. -- I assure you, my child, that your Aunt Hildegard would not tolerate. . .

HEDWIG. -- (Peremptorily) One must be still and listen to one´s conscience. You are just like all the others, Uncle Ed. I´m not sure your conscience is at peace. Has everyone a notebook? (Mumblings) All right, Gilbert, give everyone a piece of paper. We will all write what comes to us in our recollection.

STANI. -- In my day we called that "password."

HEDWIG. -- Sssh!

(Kate shakes her head and taps her forehead with her index finger.)

GEORGETTE. -- I´m not sure that our Latin minds. . .
HEDWIG. -- (To Gilbert) Don´t you have any paper?
GILBERT. -- But it´s a new box and quite expensive.
HEDWIG. -- One sheet will suffice.

(She divides it into small pieces which she distributes. A silence.)

KATE. -- (Whispers) I told you, you´d end up in an insane asylum.

(Silence. All are writing.)

HEDWIG. -- Each person will read what he or she wrote. I´m probably the only one here who writes legibly.
KATE. -- She needs a good swift kick. . .
GEORGETTE. -- Suddenly I feel intimidated. Stani?
HEDWIG. -- We´ll begin at the right.
GILBERT. -- (Reading) "I´m fed up."
MR. ZURCHER. -- "I must remember to buy some cigarettes."
KATE. -- "That black haired guy has bad breath."
GEORGETTE. -- "We haven´t seen the prospectus."
STANI. -- "One should, all the same, ask to see the prospectus."
GEORGETTE. -- Oh! Stani, I´m thrilled; our thoughts are in unison.
HEDWIG. -- "Our little quarrels dissolve into harmony as clouds into azure at the end of a beautiful summer day."
MR. ZURCHER. -- A lovely thought. I congratulate you, Hedwig.
HEDWIG. -- But I´m not happy, Uncle Ed! You had promised that you wouldn´t smoke anymore. Madame Kate, it´s kinder to pass her by in silence. And, what are these prospectus?
GEORGETTE. -- Prospectus of your father´s hotels.
HEDWIG. -- (Triumphantly) There no longer are any hotels! He sold them all. He´s going to found a colony for people who can no longer live, nor work, nor love. You can apply if you like, but there´s no guarantee that there will be a place for you.
GEORGETTE. -- (Who has gotten up) Thank you.
STANI. -- Thank you very much.

(He shakes Gil´s hand as one would at a funeral service.)

KATE. -- The footstool. (Pointing to the Dufy)
GILBERT. -- Not again!

HEDWIG. -- You want to take it with you? Don´t hesitate to. That would please me very much.

GILBERT. -- Well, I mean really. That´s a bit much. You´re not the mistress of this house yet.

HEDWIG. -- (Placidly) I´m the doctor.

MR. ZURCHER. -- I decline all responsibility. You brought me to this place where no respectable young lady would consent to stay five minutes.

HEDWIG. -- It´s no worse here than at one of your shows, Uncle Ed. It´s exactly the same sort of thing.

MR. ZURCHER. -- Furthermore, they didn´t even have the common decency to offer us a glass of water, even though it´s unbearably hot here. (To Gilbert, who protests.) No my good man, I don´t want anything. I´ll leave here having aged ten years, and tomorrow morning, when I comb my hair, it wouldn´t surprise me. . .(The ending trails off.)

(Kate, meanwhile, has taken down the painting and carries it off under her arm.)

(A silence. Hedwig remains alone with Gilbert.)

HEDWIG. -- You´ll see, you´ll come with me to the colony. There we´ll begin by living a vegetating life, like the plants. We´ll watch the cows, and then I´ll read to you aloud, I enjoy that. You´ll take a rest every day after lunch until half past three. . .We´ll lead a very restful life. . .

GILBERT. -- Yes, yes. . .only, a life that restful, I´m afraid it will kill me.

THE END

Paris, 1937

APPENDIX

GABRIEL MARCEL (1889-1973)

Dramaturge

<u>La Lumière sur la montagne</u> (1905) inédit
<u>Le Seuil Invisible</u> (1914)
  <u>La Grâce</u> (1911)
  <u>Le Palais de Sable</u> (1913)
<u>Le Quatuor en fa dièse</u> (1916-17)
<u>Un Juste</u> (1918)
<u>L'Insondable</u> (1919)
<u>Le Petit Garçon</u> (1919) inédit
Trois Pièces (1931)
  <u>Le Regard neuf</u> (1919)
  <u>La Mort de Demain</u> (1919)
  <u>La Chapelle ardente</u> (1925) (plusieurs versions 1920-25)
<u>L'Iconoclaste</u> (1920)
<u>Le Coeur des Autres</u> (1920)
<u>Un Homme de Dieu</u> (1922)
<u>L'Attelage ou le Noeud Coulant</u> (1926) inédit
<u>L'Horizon</u> (1928)
<u>Le Monde cassé</u> (1932)
<u>Le Fanal</u> (1935)
<u>Le Chemin de Crête</u> (1935)
<u>Le Dard</u> (1936)
<u>Théâtre comique</u> (1947)
  <u>Les Points sur les I</u> (1936)
  <u>Le Divertissement posthume</u> (1923)
  <u>Colombyre ou le Brasier de la Paix</u> (1937)
  <u>La Double Expertise</u> (1937)
<u>La Soif</u> (1937)
<u>Vers un autre Royaume</u> (1949)
  <u>L'Emissaire</u> (1945)
  <u>Le Signe de la Croix</u> (1938-48)
<u>La Fin des Temps</u> (1948)
<u>Rome n'est plus dans Rome</u> (1951)
<u>Mon Temps n'est plus le Votre</u> (1955)
<u>Croissiez et Multipliez</u> (1955)
<u>La Dimension Florestan</u> (1958)
<u>La Prune et la Prunelle</u> (1960)

GABRIEL MARCEL (1889-1973)

Dramatist

The Light on the Mountain (1905) unpublished
The Invisible Threshold (1914)
    Grace (1911)
    The Sand Castle (1913)
Quartet in F# (1916-17)
A Just One (1918)
The Unfathomable (1919)
The Little Boy (1919) unpublished
Three Plays (1931)
    The New Look (1919)
    Tomorrow´s Dead (1919)
    The Votive Candle (1925) (several versions 1920-25)
Rebellious Heart (1920)
The Iconoclast (1920)
A Man of God (1922)
The Yoke or the Noose (1926) unpublished
The Horizon (1928)
The Broken World (1932)
The Lantern (1935)
Ariadne (1935)
The Sting (1936)
Comic Theater (1947)
    Dot the I (1936, 6-9 nov.)
    Posthumous Joke (1923)
    Colombyre or the Torch of Peace (1937)
    The Double Expertise (1937)
Thirst (1938) reedited as Eager Hearts (1952)
Toward another Realm (1949)
    The Emissary (1945)
    The Sign of the Cross (1938-48) Epilogue (1953)
Out of Time (1950)
Rome is no longer in Rome (1951)
My time is not your time (1955)
Increase and Multiply (1955)
The Florestan Dimension (1958)
The Plum and the Apple of my Eye (1960)

*Titles not underlined have not yet been published in English.

Philosophe

Coleridge et Schelling (1909), Paris, Aubier, 1971.
Fragments philosophiques (1909-1914), Louvain et Paris, Nauwelaerts, 1961.
La Métaphysique de Royce (1917-1918), Paris, Aubier, 1945.
Journal métaphysique (1914-1923), Paris, Gallimard, 1927.
Position et approches concrètes du mystère ontologique (1933), Paris, Desclée de Brouwer 1933, Nauwelaerts, 1949, J.-M. Place, 1977.
Etre et avoir (1928-1933), Paris, Aubier, 1935.
De Refus à l'invocation , Paris, Gallimard, 1940.
Homo Viator (1941-1943), Paris, Aubier, 1945.
La Métaphysique de Royce , Paris, Aubier, 1945.
Le Mystère de l'être , 2 volumes, (1949-1950), Paris, Aubier, 1951.
Les Hommes contre l'humain , Paris, La Colombe, 1951.
Le Declin de la sagesse , Paris, Plon, 1954.
L'Homme problématique, Paris, Aubier, 1955.
Présence et immortalité (1919-1951), Paris, Flammarion, 1959.
La dignité humaine et ses assises existentielles (1961), Paris, Aubier, 1965.
Auf der Suche nach Wahrheit und Gerechtigkeit (1959-1963), Freiburg im Bresgau, Verlag Knecht, 1964.
Paix sur la terre (1964), Paris, Aubier, 1965.
Entretiens Paul Ricoeur-Gabriel Marcel, Paris, Aubier, 1968.
Pour une sagesse tragique et son au-delà, Paris, Plon, 1969.
En chemin, vers quel éveil? Paris, Gallimard, 1971.
Entretiens autour de Gabriel Marcel (1973), Neuchâtel, à la Baconnière, 1976.

Coleridge and Schelling (1909) (Preface 1967) Aubier, 1971.
Philosophical Fragments (1909-1914) Nauwelaerts, 1961; University of Notre Dame Press, 1965.
Royce's Metaphysics (1917-1918) Montaigne, 1945; Regnery, 1956, 1975.
Metaphysical Journal (1914-1923) Gallimard, 1927; Chicago, H. Regnery, 1952.
On the Ontological Mystery (1932) Desclee de Brouwer, 1933; Nauwelaerts 1949; J.-M. Place, 1977; pp. 9-46 in The Philosophy of Existentialism: Secaucus,N.J., The Citadel Press, 1956.
Being and Having (1928-1953) Aubier, 1935; New York, Harper and Row, 1965.
Creative Fidelity , Gallimard, 1940; New York, Farrar, Straus and Co., 1964.
Homo Viator (1941-1944), Aubier, 1945; Homo Viator , New York, Harper and Bros., 1962; available Peter Smith, 6 Lexington Ave., Magnolia, MA 01930, 1978.
The Mystery of Being , 2 vols. (1949-50), Aubier, 1951; Chicago, H. Regnery, 1962, Lanham, Maryland, University Press of America, 1984.
Man against Mass Society , La Colombe, 1951; Fayard, 1968; Chicago, H. Regnery, 1962.
The Decline of Wisdom , Plon, 1954; London, Harvill Press, 1954; New York, Philosophical Library, 1955.
Problematic Man , Aubier, 1955; New York, Herder and Herder, 1967.
Presence and Immortality (1919-1951) Flammarion, 1959; Pittsburgh, Pa., Duquesne University Press, 1967; Louvain, Ed. Nauwelaerts, 1967.
Searchings (1959-1965), Freiburg im Bresgau, Verlag Knecht, 1964; New York, Paulist Newman Press, 1967.
The Existential Background of Human Dignity , (1961), Cambridge, Mass., Harvard University Press, 1963; Paris, Aubier, 1965.
"The Philosopher and Peace" (1964), in Philosophical Fragments and The Philosopher and Peace, Notre Dame, Indiana, University of Notre Dame Press, 1965.
Conversations between Paul Ricoeur and Gabriel Marcel , Aubier, 1968, included in Tragic Wisdom and Beyond , Plon, 1969; Northwestern University Press, 1973.
"An Autobiographical Essay" (Spring 1969) in The Philosophy of Gabriel Marcel , (The Library of Living Philosophers, Vol. XVII) ed. P. A. Schilpp and L. E. Hahn, LaSalle, Illinois, Open Court, 1984.
En route, Toward What an Awakening? , Gallimard 1971.
Conversations around Gabriel Marcel , (1973), Neuchatel, a la Baconniere, 1976.

* Dates in parentheses are dates of composition. Dates not in parentheses are dates of publication.

Critique dramatique

Théâtre et religion, Paris, Vitte, 1958.
L'Heure théâtrale. De Giraudoux à Jean-Paul Sartre, Paris, Plon, 1959.
Regards sur le théâtre de Claudel, Paris, Beauchesne, 1964.

Cf. Bibliography of Drama Reviews in Roger Troisfontaines, *De l'existence à l'être. La Philosophie de Gabriel Marcel*, 2e vol., pp. 385-422.

Drama criticism

Theater and Religion, Paris, Vitte, 1958.
The Theater Hour, Paris, Plon, 1958.
A Review of Paul Claudel's Theater, Paris, Beauchesne, 1964.

Cf. Bibliography of Drama Reviews in Roger Troisfrontaines, De l'existence à l'être. La Philosophie de Gabriel Marcel, 2e vol., pp. 385-422.

"The Drama of the Soul in Exile," Preface to Three Plays by Gabriel Marcel, New York, Hill and Wang, 1965.

"My Dramatic Works as Viewed by the Philosopher," in Searchings, New York, Newman Press, 1967.

The Existential Background of Human Dignity, Cambridge, MA., Harvard University Press, 1963.

"Introduction" to Existential Drama of Gabriel Marcel, West Hartford, CT., McAuley Institute, 1974.

Recent Reeditions of Marcel's Plays in French

Cinq Pièces Majeures: Un Homme de Dieu, Le Monde cassé, Le Chemin de crête, La Soif, Le Signe de la croix, Paris, Plon, 1973.
Le Secret est dans les Iles: Le Dard, L'Emissaire, La Fin des Temps, Paris, Plon, 1967.
Percées vers un ailleurs: L'Iconoclaste, L'Horizon, Paris, Fayard, 1973.

Plays by Marcel Published in English Versions

Three Plays by Gabriel Marcel: Ariadne, A Man of God, Votive Candle, New York, Hill and Wang, 1965.
Existential Drama of Gabriel Marcel, The Broken World, The Rebellious Heart, West Hartford, Conn., McAuley Institute, 1974.
The Lantern in Cross Currents, Spring, 1958.
The Unfathomable in Presence and Immortality, Pittsburgh, Pa., Duquesne University Press, 1967.
Two One Act Plays by Gabriel Marcel: Dot the I, and The Double Expertise, Lanham, Maryland, University Press of America, 1985.

GABRIEL MARCEL BIBLIO-BIOGRAPHY

1889 Born December 7 in Paris.

1893 November 15, death of his mother, born Laure Meyer, July 30, 1866.

1898 His father, Henry Marcel, married Marguerite Meyer, sister of the first wife, before going to Stockholm as ambassador. They stayed in Sweden 1898-1899 until Henry Marcel returned to Paris to fill the post of Minister of Fine Arts.

1904 Submitted to Fernand Gregh a play in the style of Ibsen that was a childish presentiment of A Man of God.

1909 Friends at the Sorbonne with Jacques Rivière, Henri Franck and Jean Wahl. Degree conferred with the submission of "The metaphysical ideas of Coleridge and their connection with the philosophy of Schelling." Followed the lectures of Henri Bergson, who taught at the Collège de France.

1910 Agrégation de philosophie.

1911 Taught at Lycée de Vendôme.

1912-13 Taught in a small private school above Lake Geneva.

1914 Began writing his Metaphysical Journal. Published his first plays: Paris, Ed. Grasset, Le Seuil Invisible: Preface, La Grâce, Le Palais de Sable (The Invisible Threshold: Preface, Grace, The Sand Castle). During the war, he directed a Red Cross Center in Paris and an information service on those missing in action.

1915-18 Taught at Lycée Condorcêt in Paris.

1916-17 Metapsychical experiences.

1919 Married Jacqueline Boegner.

1919-23 Professor at Sens.

1921 Le Coeur des Autres (Rebellious Heart) published (Theatre: Ed. Grasset).

1922 Encounter with Charles Du Bos, whom he succeeded as editor of Plon´s Collection "Feux Croisés."

1923 Settled in Paris, 21 rue de Tournon. Worked with Nouvelle Revue Francaise, and became dramatic and then literary critic for L´Europe Nouvelle. L´Iconoclaste (The Iconoclast) published (Théâtre: Ed. Stock).

1925 Le Quatuor en fa dièse (Quartet in F#) published (Théâtre: Ed. Stock). Un Homme de Dieu (A Man of God published.

1926 March 6. Death of his father, Henry Marcel, who was born November 1854.

1927 Publication of Journal Métaphysique (Metaphysical Journal)(Ed. Gallimard).

1929 Religious experience and conversion. Baptised March 23 with François Mauriac as sponsor.

1931 Published Trois pièces: Le Regard neuf, Le Mort de demain, La Chapelle ardente (Plon),(Three Plays: The New Look, Tomorrow´s Dead, The Votive Candle).

1933 Le Monde cassé (The Broken World) published (Théâtre: Ed. Desclée de Brouwer), followed by the essay "Position et approches concrète du mystère ontologique" ("On the Ontological Mystery").

1935 Etre et avoir (Being and Having) published (Aubier).

1936 Le Chemin de crête, Ariadne published (Théâtre: Ed. Grasset). Le Dard (The Sting) published (Théâtre: Ed. Plon).

1938 La Soif (Thirst)(Théâtre: Ed. Desclée de Brouwer) reedited under the title Les Coeurs avides (Eager Hearts) (La Table Ronde, 1952).

1939-40 Taught at Lycée Louis-le-Grand.

1940 Death of Henry Marcel´s second wife Marguerite, who raised Gabriel Marcel. Published Du Refus à l´invocation (Creative Fidelity) (Gallimard). Acquired the Chateau de Peuch in Corrèze, where the family lived from 1941-1943.

1941 Taught several months at Lycée de Montpellier.

1944 Became drama critic for Nouvelles Littéraires. Before the war he worked for several reviews, L'Europe Nouvelle, La Nouvelle Revue Francaise, Sept, Temps présent, La Vie intellectuelle, etc.

1945 L'Horizon (The Horizon) published (Théâtre; Edition des Etudiants de France). Homo Viator (Homo Viator) published (Aubier). La Métaphysique de Royce (Royce's Metaphysics) published (Aubier). For the years 1945 through 1947 music was at the center of creative activities.

1947 Death of his wife. Apercus phénoménologiques sur l'être en situation (Phenomenological notes on being in a situation) (Boivin). Théâtre Comique: Colombyre, ou le Brasier de la Paix; La Double Expertise; Les Points sur les I; Le Divertissement posthume. (Comic Theater: Colombyre, or the Torch of Peace, The Double Expertise, Dot the I, The Posthumous Joke.) (Albin Michel). Existentialisme Chrétien (Christian Existentialism) (Plon, collection "Présences" in collaboration with Etienne Gilson, Jeanne Delhomme, Roger Troisfontaines, Pierre Colin, J.-P. Dubois-Dumée).

1948 Directed a UNESCO conference at Beyrouth.

1949 Received the Grand Prize for Literature from the French Academy. Published Vers un autre Royaume: L'Emissaire; Le Signe de la Croix, (Toward another World: The Emissary, The Sign of the Cross). (Théâtre: Ed. Plon). Delivered the Gifford Lectures at University of Aberdeen, Scotland, The Mystery of Being, I. Reflection and Mystery, II. Faith and Reality.

1950 La Fin des temps (The End of Time) Théâtre: Réalités.

1951 Le Mystère de l'être, (The Mystery of Being,) 2 vols. (Aubier). Rome n'est plus dans Rome (Rome Is No Longer in Rome) (Théâtre: Ed. de La Table Ronde). Les Hommes contre l'humain (Man Against Mass Society) (La Colombe). Travel in North Africa, then in South America.

1952 Elected a Member of the Institute of France, Academy of Political and Moral Sciences.

1953 Le Declin de la sagesse (The Decline of Wisdom) (Plon).

1954 L'Homme problématique (Problematic Man) (Aubier).

1955 <u>Mon temps n´est pas le vôtre</u> (My Time is not Your Time) (Théâtre: Ed. Plon). <u>Croissez et multipliez</u> (Increase and multiply) (Théâtre: Ed. Plon).

1956 Received the Goethe Prize from the town of Hamburg, conferred in Germany for one who fosters a supranational spirit and work in favor of humanity.

1956-66 Numerous trips in the United States and Canada and to Japan where he was received by the emperor.

1958 Received the National Grand Prize for Literature. <u>La Dimension Florestan,</u> "Le Crepuscule du sens commun," (The Florestan Dimension,) "The Twilight of Common Sense" (Plon).

1959 <u>Présence et immortalité,</u> (<u>Presence and Immortality.</u> (Flammarion) <u>L´Heure théâtrale</u> (The Theater Hour) (Plon).

1960 <u>La Prune et la prunelle,</u> (L´Avant scene). (The Plum and the Apple of My Eye).

1961 Delivered the William James Lectures at Harvard University. <u>The Existential Background of Human Dignity.</u>

1963 Received the Osiris Prize. <u>The Existential Background of Human Dignity,</u> Harvard University Press.

1964 Received the Frankfurt Peace Prize, conferred by German editors, publishers, and book dealers. <u>Auf der Suche nach Wahrheit und Gerechtigkeit,</u> (<u>Searchings</u>) ed. Wolfgang Ruf, Freiburg im Bresgau, Verlag Knecht. <u>Regards sur le theatre de Claudel</u> , (Reviews of Paul Claudel´s Theater), (Beauchesne).

1965 Delivered the opening discourse at the Salzburg Music Festival. <u>Paix sur la terre</u> (Peace on Earth) (Aubier). Lectures in the United States.

1967 <u>Le Secret est dans les îles</u> (The Secret is in the Isles) (Plon).

1968 <u>Entretiens Paul Ricoeur, Gabriel Marcel</u> (<u>Conversations between Paul Ricoeur and Gabriel Marcel</u>) (Aubier).

1969 Received the Erasmus Prize. "An Autobiographical Essay" (1969) in <u>The Philosophy of Gabriel Marcel,</u> La Salle, Open Court, 1984. Visited Dresden and Prague.

1971 Le Siècle à venir, (The Century to Come) Fondation Roland de Jouvenel. Pour une sagesse tragique et son au-delà, (Tragic Wisdom and Beyond) (Plon). En chemin, vers quel eveil? (En Route Toward What an Awakening?) (Gallimard). Coleridge et Schelling (Coleridge and Schelling) (Aubier).

1972 Received the Dignity of the Grand Cross of the National Order of Merit of the Legion of Honor, of which he was already an Officer and a Commander.

1973 Percées vers un ailleurs (Breakthrough Toward a Beyond) (Fayard). Cinq Pièces Majeures (Five Major Plays) (Plon). Colloquium at Cerisy la Salle, International Cultural Center, Aug. 24-31, 1973, discussing his theater and philosophy.

1973 October 8. Died in Paris.

1975 Foundation of an international association, Présence de Gabriel Marcel, which groups his family, friends, and associates and continues the study of his work. Social Center: 85 boulevard de Port-Royal, Paris, 75013. Secrétariat: 9 avenue Franklin-Roosevelt, Paris 75008.

1976 Entretiens autour de Gabriel Marcel (Conversations Around Gabriel Marcel) (Neuchâtel, à la Baconnière). Proceedings of 1973 international colloquium on the Theater and Philosophy of Gabriel Marcel, published with the sponsorship of the European Cultural Foundation, 9 avenue Franklin-Roosevelt, Paris 75008, France.

1977 Gabriel Marcel interrogé par Pierre Boutang, (Gabriel Marcel interviewed by Pierre Boutang) (Archives du XXe Siècle) Editions J.-M. Place, 1978. Followed by a reedition of "Position et approches concrètes du mystère ontologique," ("On the Ontological Mystery").

Sources for Biographic and biblio-biographic information:

Louis Chaigne, Vie et oeuvres d'écrivains, (Life and Works of Writers), Vol. 4, F. Lanore, 1954, pp. 183-201.

Jeanne Parain-Vial, Gabriel Marcel et les niveaux de l'expérience, (Gabriel Marcel and the levels of experience)Seghers, 1966, Biblio-biographie, pp. 99-107.

Gabriel Marcel interrogé par Pierre Boutang, (Gabriel Marcel Interviewed by Pierre Boutang) J.-M. Place Ed., 1978, p. 116.

Biblio-biography of Gabriel Marcel´s Entrance into the English-Speaking World.

1949 The Philosophy of Existence, London, Harvill Press, 1949; New York, The Philosophical Library, 1949; Freeport, New York, Books for Libraries Press, 1969 reprint of 1949 edition. English version of "Positions et approches concrètes du mystère ontologique."

Being and Having, Westminister, Dacre Press, 1949; New York, Harper and Row, 1965.

1949-50 Gifford Lectures at Aberdeen University, Scotland.

1950 The Mystery of Being. Vol. I. Reflection and Mystery. Vol. II. Faith and Reality. London, Harvill Press, 1950-51; Chicago, Regnery/Gateway, 1960; Lanham, Maryland, University Press of America, 1984.

1951 Homo Viator, London, V. Gollanoz, 1951; Chicago, H. Regnery Co., 1951; New York, Harper and Row, 1962; Peter Smith, Magnolia, Mass. 1978.

1952 Three Plays by Gabriel Marcel, A Man of God, Ariadne, and The Votive Candle (The Funeral Pyre), London, Secker and Warburg, 1952; New York, Hill and Wang, 1965. Includes preface "The Drama of the Soul in Exile" (A lecture given in July 1950 by Gabriel Marcel at L´Institut Français in London).

Metaphysical Journal, Chicago, H. Regnery Co., 1952; London, Rockliff Press, 1952, with essay "Existence and Objectivity" in appendix.

Man Against Mass Society, London, Harvill Press, 1952; Chicago, H. Regnery, 1952; Gateway edition, 1962.

1954 The Decline of Wisdom, London, Harvill Press, 1954; New York, The Philosophical Library, 1955; and Chicago, H. Regnery, 1955.

1956 The Philosophy of Existentialism, New York, The Philosophical Library, The Citadel Press Inc., 1956; 1961.

Royce´s Metaphysics, Chicago, H. Regnery Co., 1956; 1975.

1958 The Lantern in Cross Currents, West Nyack, New York, 1958.

1961 The William James Lectures delivered at Harvard University.

1963 The Existential Background of Human Dignity, Cambridge, Mass., Harvard University Press, 1963.

1964 Creative Fidelity, New York, Farrar, Straus, and Co., 1964.

1964-65 Lectures and travel throughout the United States and Canada.

1965 Philosophical Fragments (1904-1914) and The Philosopher and Peace, Notre Dame, Indiana, Notre Dame University Press, 1965.

1967 Problematic Man, New York, Herder and Herder, 1967.

Presence and Immortality, Pittsburgh, Pa., Duquesne University Press, 1967. Includes The Unfathomable, the first act of an unfinished play. (1919).

Searchings, New York, Paulist-Newman Press, 1967. Includes "My Dramatic Works as Viewed by the Philosopher" (1959).

1973 Conversations between Paul Ricoeur and Gabriel Marcel included in Tragic Wisdom and Beyond, Evanston, Illinois, Northwestern University Press, 1973.

1974 The Existentialist Drama of Gabriel Marcel: The Broken World, The Rebellious Heart and an Introduction by Gabriel Marcel, ed. F. J. Lescoe, West Hartford, Conn., McAuley Institute, St. Joseph College, 1974.

1984 "An Autobiographical Essay" in The Philosophy of Gabriel Marcel, (The Library of Living Philosophers, Vol. XVII), ed. P. A. Schilpp and L. E. Hahn, LaSalle, Illinois, Open Court, 1984.

1986 Two One Act Plays by Gabriel Marcel: Dot the I, and The Double Expertise. Introduction by Jean-Marie and Anne Marcel, Lanham, Maryland, University Press of America, 1986.

Biographical and Bibliographical References

Biographical data on Gabriel Marcel may be found in:

Gabriel Marcel, "An Essay in Autobiography" in The Philosophy of Existentialism , Secaucus, New Jersey, The Citadel Press, 1956, pp. 104-28. En Chemin, vers quel eveil? (En Route Toward What an Awakening?) Paris, Gallimard, 1971. "An Autobiographical Essay" (Spring 1969) in The Philosophy of Gabriel Marcel (Library of Living Philosophers Vol. XVII) ed. Paul A. Schilpp and Lewis E. Hahn, LaSalle, Illinois, Open Court, 1984, pp. 3-68.

H. J. Blackham, Six Existentialist Thinkers, London, Routledge and Kegan Paul, 1951.

I. M. Bochenski, Contemporary European Thought, Berkeley, California, University of California Press, 1956.

Seymour Cain, Gabriel Marcel. New York, Hillary House, 1963; South Bend, Indiana, Regnery/Gateway, 1979.

Kenneth T. Gallagher, The Philosophy of Gabriel Marcel, New York, Fordham University Press, 1962, 1975.

Samuel Keen, Gabriel Marcel . Richmond, Virginia, John Knox Press, 1967.

Francis J. Lescoe, Existentialism with or without God , New York, Alba House, 1974.

Vincent P. Miceli, Ascent to Being. Gabriel Marcel´s Philosophy of Communion , New York, Tournai, Paris, Rome, Desclée, 1965.

David Roberts, Existentialism and Religious Belief , New York, Oxford University Press, 1957.

Herbert Spiegelberg, The Phenomenological Movement, A Historical Introduction . 2 vols., The Hague, Martinus Nijhoff, 1960.

Roger Troisfontaines, De l´existence a l´etre . La Philosophie de Gabriel Marcel , Louvain, Nauwelaerts; Paris, Vrin, 1952; 1965.

Bibliographical data on Gabriel Marcel may be found in:

François H. Lapointe, "A Bibliography of the Writings of Gabriel Marcel," pp. 583-609 in The Philosophy of Gabriel Marcel , (Library of Living Philosophers Vol. XVII), ed. P. A. Schilpp and L. E. Hahn, LaSalle, Illinois, Open Court, 1984.

François H. Lapointe and Claire C. Lapointe, Gabriel Marcel and His Critics: An International Bibliography (1928-1976) , New York and London, Garland Publishing Inc., 1977.

Roger Troisfontaines, De l'existence à l'être . La Philosophie de Gabriel Marcel , (From Existence to Being . The Philosophy of Gabriel Marcel), Louvain, Nauwelaerts; Paris, Vrin, 1952, 1965. Volume II. pp. 381-464.

Compiled by Katharine Rose Hanley

Two One Act Plays by Gabriel Marcel offers a brief, but representative, sampling in English of the theater of this French existentialist writer. The book presents *The Double Expertise* , a light-hearted comedy, and *Dot the I* , a play with comic dimensions that ends in poignant drama.

These are the first of Marcel´s comedies to be published in English, and make a total of nine of his thirty plays available to readers of English. The book, moreover, offers a comedy and a drama that can easily be staged in brief periods of time.

An introduction by Jean-Marie and Anne Marcel and a translator´s preface by Katharine Rose Hanley help set the stage for readers´ enjoyment of the plays.

The book concludes with significant information about Gabriel Marcel´s life and works that will be valuable to Marcel scholars and also of practical interest to anyone desiring to know more about Marcel (1889-1973) and his writings.

Dot the I and *The Double Expertise* originally appeared in French under the titles, *Les points sur les I* and *La Double Expertise* , and were published along with *Colombyre ou le brasier de la paix* (*Colombyre or the Torch of Peace*) and *Le Divertissement posthume* (*The Posthumous Joke*) in *Théâtre comique* by Gabriel Marcel, Paris, Albin Michel, 1947.

About The Translator

Katharine Rose Hanley is a Professor of Philosophy at Le Moyne College, Syracuse, New York, where she has taught since 1961. Since 1975 she has also served there as director of the Gabriel Marcel Institute for Existential Drama.

Her interest in theater springs from involvement with ballet in the Young People's Dance Theater of New Jersey, 1943-48. Her enthusiasm for languages also dates from early childhood. She pursued studies of language and then philosophy at St. Elizabeth's Academy, New Jersey; Manhattanville College, New York; Laval University, Quebec, Canada; Heidelberg University, Germany; and Louvain University, Belgium.

She received her Ph.D. in Philosophy from the Higher Institute of Philosophy, Louvain University, Belgium, July 4, 1961. Since that time she has published essays in metaphysics as well as numerous articles pertaining to Gabriel Marcel's thought. Her recent studies of Gabriel Marcel's theater and philosophy have brought her invitations to address the international association Présence de Gabriel Marcel and the Société française de Philosophie, in Paris, France, January-February, 1984.